American Hotel Story

Also by Richard Estep

In Search of the Paranormal
Serial Killers
The World's Most Haunted Hospitals
The Farnsworth House Haunting
Trail of Terror
Colorado UFOs
The Devil's Coming to Get Me
The Fairfield Haunting
Haunted Healthcare
The Horrors of Fox Hollow Farm
Building the Write Life

As co-author

The Haunting of Asylum 49
Spirits of the Cage
The Black Monk of Pontefract

American Hotel Story

History, Hauntings, and Heartbreak in LA's
Infamous Hotel Cecil

Richard Estep

For Tim Schoon.

You were the best of us.

In addition to interviews, many of the times, dates, and facts contained in this book were drawn from primary sources, mostly contemporary newspaper reports. Where accounts differ, attempts have been made to reconcile names, dates, times, and locations by cross-checking multiple sources. I have striven for accuracy, but any errors in this book are strictly my own.

—RE

Foreword

My friendship with my fellow ghost writer Richard Estep was forged after an online booking mishap at an allegedly haunted inn located next to Edith Wharton's The Mount in Lenox, Massachusetts.

It was September 2019 and I invited him to be a guest speaker at a convention that I produced called *Mass ParaCon,* and I was under the assumption that I had secured a multi-room "carriage house" for myself, Richard, and our demonologist friend James Annitto. The photos from the inn's website were a bit misleading and, to be candid, we were cramped in a small room with two beds and a makeshift cot for the entire weekend.

As soon as we arrived, I tried my best to find him his own private accomodations at the recently renovated hotel. No luck. The overnight haunt was completely sold out and we were stuck together in a cramped room for three days in the Berkshires.

What could have been a paranormal convention nightmare turned into a "happy accident" as Richard and I chatted into the wee hours of the night. While we were trying to get some much-needed shut eye, I opened up a sneak peek clip on my computer from a show that I had just filmed, discussing Salem's Lady in the Blue Dress for the Travel Channel's *Most Terrifying Places*.

"Did you just say 'in the *bowels* of the Rockefeller building?'" he asked, with his familiar British accent that I recognized from his work on *Haunted Case Files* and *Paranormal 911*. I sheepishly nodded my head "yes," expecting him to eviscerate me for being too over the top. "Great choice of words. I like it."

We then started to talk about our experiences with various publishing groups and filming television shows for the Travel Channel and, ultimately, came to the conclusion that we had a similar passion for storytelling, specifically in print. We both agreed that our stints on television were merely a flash in the pan and our true purpose in life was to continue to write the books that we're both known for in the paranormal field.

What I liked most about our heart-to-heart conversation was his strong stance on the importance of historical accuracy and our mutual disdain of the aggressive male psyche approach to provoking spirits on camera just because it usually solicits a response.

I then asked him about using people as trigger objects, or

"human bait" as I crassly worded it, and we discussed his work investigating serial killer Herb Baumeister for his book, *The Horrors of Fox Hollow Farm*. He gave me some behind-the-scenes intel about the case and I quickly learned that Richard and I not only shared space on Amazon's "Ghosts & Hauntings" bestseller list, but we also had a similar code of ethics.

Richard and I were on the same page, both literally and figuratively.

To be honest, the serendipitous nature of our ghost writer relationship can be downright shocking at times. For example, we both started writing about true crime and the paranormal at the same time. My book, *Mass Murders*, was about the historical crimes in my home state of Massachusetts. When I investigated the Stanley Hotel in Estes Park, Colorado years ago for my book, *Ghost Writers*, the tour guide kept referring to her mentor "Sir Richard," who wrote paranormal-themed books. Yes, she was talking about the one and only Richard Estep. When I decided to create an audiobook version of my *Haunted Hotels of New England* manuscript, I was surprised to learn that out of hundreds of potential narrators available, we both chose the same voiceover artist, Ronald Fox.

Weird coincidences? Yes, and that's just the beginning.

We also recently both penned books about the Revolutionary War and, get this, the title of this project, *American Hotel Story*, is almost identical to the working title of a book deal I pitched months ago called *American Ghost Story*. And, no, we both didn't share details about our projects until after the contract was signed and he did a cover reveal.

Seriously, some of the similarities can be downright uncanny. But I don't view Richard as a competitor. He is, in my opinion, the go-to author in the paranormal field for single-location investigations. My books are often regional in scope and encompass several historical haunts. Our work is complimentary on many levels and I find that we are often paired together without even trying.

When we both were asked to be featured guests at the Gettysburg Battlefield Bash in a sea of vendor tables, organizers set us up right next to each other. We had a blast being paracon neighbors. After previously appearing on The Dark Zone's live streaming event at the Lizzie Borden B&B in Fall River, producers created pairings and put us on screen together to discuss the *RMS Queen Mary* in Long Beach, California without even knowing that we were friends.

For the record, we were a great team. I've worked the graveyard shift at various hotels with reported hauntings and Richard has worked in the medical field, so we were able to give an insightful perspective on the *Queen Mary*'s hauntings based on our areas of expertise.

Our appearances on television also often overlap. The producers of *Haunted Case Files* wanted to feature an author who incorporates paranormal investigations for their show. While I laboriously auditioned for the program, they ended up choosing Richard because he had a lot of tangible evidence that would work well for the format. The casting ended up being a blessing in disguise because I filmed the 100th episode of *A Haunting* soon after and the program called "Provoking Evil" was a career-changing move for me.

A Haunting also led to several programs chronicling my paranormal experiences in Salem, Massachusetts. A few months after Richard and I bonded in the Berkshires, we were contacted by Bristow Media Group about a new TV program called *Paranormal Nightshift*. Richard had served as an expert on several of the Canadian production group's shows including *Haunted Hospitals* and *Paranormal 911*. They reached out to me to recount a terrifying experience I had with an entity working the overnight shift at a hotel in

Salem.

Producers, of course, paired us together and the result was their highest rated episode that aired on the Travel Channel, called "Family Secret."

What I liked the most about working with Richard on the program is that he actually called me from the set to clarify some of the specifics about my case. "Sam, it says here that the entity had red glowing eyes," he asked me. "Is that true?"

Unfortunately, it was, and the face-to-face encounter has haunted me for years. I then talked about how the case has been a mystery to me because I wasn't sure if it had anything to do with my family lineage. After spending years giving tours in the Witch City and writing two books on Salem's hauntings, I learned from my mother that I was related to the Putnams, the major accusers during the witch hysteria of 1692 that resulted in the execution of twenty innocent men and women.

Was the entity an innocent victim of the Salem Witch Trials or something more sinister like a hat-wearing shadow figure? I appreciated Richard's questions before weighing in on my case and the finished product was one of my favorite appearances on television.

While we have different approaches to the paranormal,

the bottom line is that we respect each other. I'm a former journalist who also happens to identify as a clairvoyant. Richard is a medical professional who has decades of experience as a paranormal investigator. There's the obvious geographical difference. He's based in Colorado and I'm in New England. And, for those who haven't heard Richard's charming British accent, he's originally from across the pond and I'm a Southern boy from the Florida panhandle who relocated to Boston in the 1990s.

When he asked me to write the foreword to *American Hotel Story*, I didn't skip a beat. Yes, I was also working on a book that had a chapter chronicling the ghost lore and serial killers associated with the notorious hotel in the middle of Skid Row in Los Angeles, but I know that we have a similar mission. Our goal is to untangle the many myths and misconceptions associated with the Hotel Cecil and it was important to both of us not to sensationalize the mysterious death of Elisa Lam.

If there's one thing that I've learned about my friend and colleague that separates him from the misguided paranormal investigators on TV and now the various streaming platforms, it's that Richard Estep tells the truth. And with *American Hotel Story*, he reaffirms Mark Twain's old adage once again ... the truth is stranger than fiction.

Sam Baltrusis is the author of thirteen paranormal-themed books including "Ghosts of the American Revolution." Richard Estep and Sam Baltrusis are currently hashing out several collaborations including a book on the hauntings associated with the USS Salem *in Quincy, Massachusetts. For more information, visit SamBaltrusis.com.*

Introduction

Every hotel has its ghost story.

I should know. I used to work in one. The hotel that inspired Stephen King to write arguably the greatest of his timeless and terrifying novels. I gave ghost tours to the thousands of tourists who flocked there each year, most of them looking for a few chills, some creepy stories, and perhaps even a brush with something otherworldly.

If I hadn't believed in ghosts before I started working there, I would have been left in no doubt when I left three years later. Strange events were close to everyday occurrences, particularly on the top floor and in the concert hall, which looked little different than it had when the place first opened more than a hundred years before.

My friends and colleagues in the tour department were — and still are, I believe — the keepers of the ghostly lore; not only those that went back many years, but also the weird experiences that countless guests would frequently approach them to share.

Nor was this hotel particularly unusual in that regard. During the quarter of a century that I have spent as a paranormal investigator, researching claims of ghostly phenomena and haunted locations, it seems as though almost every hotel I visit has a resident specter or two. Not all of them want those stories to be known to the general public — rumors of a haunting can be both good *and* bad for business — but they are there nonetheless. Visitors from a bygone age which sometimes intrude upon our own.

Which brings us to the Hotel Cecil. Or the Cecil Hotel. Take your pick; it has been called both during its long and tangled lifetime.

One can hardly look anywhere online or on TV these days without seeing something related to the Cecil. The tragic death of Elisa Lam in 2013 catapulted the hotel onto the global stage, thanks mainly to the eerie video footage of her acting strangely in an elevator just before she disappeared under mysterious circumstances. This, in turn, inspired the makers of the popular TV show *American Horror Story* to base their fifth season, titled *Hotel*, on the Cecil. Their fictional Hotel Cortez is a thinly veiled Cecil clone, frequented by a host of dark and terrifying characters — and host to a phantom serial killers' get together. Present at that malign gathering is one Richard Ramirez, the infamous "Night Stalker" who terrorized Californians with a spree of horrific crimes during the 1980s. Ramirez had an established relationship with the Cecil, having lived out of a room on the fourteenth floor prior to his arrest, and the show's creator, Ryan Murphy, admits to having a fascination with what is arguably L.A.'s most infamous hotel.

Long before claims of the Cecil being haunted entered the mainstream, serial killer aficionados flocked to the hotel because of its link to Ramirez and another, lesser-known serial killer, Jack Unterweger.

Interest in the Cecil peaked again in early 2021 with the release of two TV shows. One was a Netflix true crime documentary titled *Crime Scene: The Vanishing at the Cecil Hotel*. Produced by renowned Hollywood director Ron Howard, the show spends four episodes looking into the bizarre circumstances surrounding Elisa Lam's disappearance and death.

The second was in a rather different vein. The paranormal reality show *Ghost Adventures* featured the Cecil in a two-hour special, in which they were given exclusive behind the scenes access to the currently shut down hotel, in order to conduct their own unique brand of exploration.

In an interview with *People.com*[1], host Zak Bagans said he wanted to explore the possibility that Elisa Lam had been influenced to take her own life by a dark entity of some kind, possibly one that was conjured by Richard Ramirez in an occult ritual that was supposedly performed on the hotel's rooftop.

Bagans also says that *"you could feel these spirits move through you, around you, they're watching you."*

It must be pointed out that *Ghost Adventures* is a show that seems to find a haunting of some description everywhere it goes, and the vast majority of them are described as being dark or malevolent in nature. That does not necessarily mean that Bagans is wrong, however. The Cecil and the area around it have a long history of negative events, such as violence, suicide, drug abuse, and prostitution. Is it possible that tangible elements of that negativity have manifested in the building somehow, in the form of a type of energy which we do not yet understand?

The more I looked into the Hotel Cecil and its history, the more questions I had about the place. This book is my attempt to answer some of them.

Readers and listeners should be cautioned that this is not the usual type of book I would write. For one thing, it is significantly shorter than most of my projects. That's because wherever possible, I prefer to visit a location in person, conducting my own research on site with a small team of trusted colleagues. That was not possible this time out. Not only did the Covid 19 pandemic prevent us from traveling, but the owners of the Cecil will no longer allow paranormal investigators inside. According to Bagans, his TV shoot is the only time that an investigation will ever be allowed inside the old hotel. It is currently in the process of being remodeled and given a new lease of life, a different image, in the hopes of breaking away from the Cecil's dark past.

All of which means that this book is mostly a work of didactic research. Despite my best efforts, I was unable to walk the hallways of the Cecil myself, so I did the next best thing: I talked to a man who has, a fellow investigator who visited the hotel on several occasions to check out the claims of paranormal activity for himself. I also played armchair researcher, delving into decades worth of historical documentation and old newspaper archives. I wanted to learn more about the poor unfortunate souls who had died within the Cecil's walls, or on the sidewalk outside.

I went down a lot of rabbit holes during that process. The Internet hosts hundreds of conspiracy theories concerning the disappearance and death of Elisa Lam, and just as many fanciful tales concerning everything from the occult to serial killers. I'm frankly surprised not to have found anything to do with aliens, though perhaps I just didn't look hard enough.

When the dust finally settled, I found as many questions as I did potential answers. In many ways, I'm as much in the dark about certain aspects of the hotel and the events which took place there as I was at the very beginning.

The truth is that in attempting to tell the story of the Hotel Cecil, I have found more history than haunting about which to write. Yet the Cecil's story is still a compelling one, and I can only hope that I have done it some kind of justice within these pages.

Let's go and find out, shall we?

Richard Estep
Longmont, Colorado
March 2021

(note: I have included the titles of appropriate newspaper sources as they are referenced in the text)

[1] https://people.com/tv/ghost-adventures-zak-bagans-on-poltergeist-activity-at-cecil-hotel/

CHAPTER ONE
Skid Row

Located on the east side of Main Street, downtown Los Angeles, between 6th and 7th Streets, the Hotel Cecil was designed by the esteemed architect Loy Lester Smith (1885-1956). It was originally conceived as the Metropolitan Hotel, and cost over $1,000,000 to construct during the early 1920s.

Little expense was spared in outfitting the newcomer to L.A.'s hotel scene. A set of bespoke walnut dressers which, if placed end to end in one continuous line, would have measured a half mile long, was manufactured by a Los Angeles-based firm called the Roberts-Cohen Company. The dressers were just a small part of the 4,000 pieces of furniture that the Cecil required, the installation of which was to be overseen by the reputable Barker Brothers. All told, the furniture took more than a hundred truck loads to deliver.

The furnishing scheme of the Cecil was planned with a view to giving unstinted comfort and content to the guests who sojourn beneath its roof, read a self-congratulatory advertisement that Barker Brothers took out in the *Los Angeles Times*. They really had gone all-out, ensuring that every single piece of furnishing was custom made, right down to the elegant woven carpets and even the individual bedside lamps.

The hotel first opened its doors on December 20, 1924. The Roaring Twenties had not yet come to an end, and there was no shortage of cash being splashed around in the City of Angels. The Cecil's marketing literature trumpeted: *14 Stories Absolutely Fireproof*, implying grandeur and safety all in the same sentence. The Cecil would cater to businessmen, bankers, accountants, and a host of other professionals. L.A.'s Spring Street financial district was within easy walking distance. Known as the Wall Street of the West, affluence poured into the area, and some of it inevitably found its way into the hotel's coffers.

The Broadway theater district was also just two blocks away, so audiences could take in an evening show and then spend a night at the Cecil. So too could stars, directors, and the crews of movies that were shooting their latest production in and around Hollywood. The Cecil stood through the great Hollywood transition from stage-based theater to first silent and then, finally, talking motion pictures.

The hotel was comprised of some seven hundred rooms.

Of this number, the lion's share (three hundred) were shared, or communal bathrooms, and were priced at an economical but not exactly cheap $1.50 per night. Moving up the scale, $2.00 per night would get you one of the two hundred rooms which had its own toilet, though you still had to share a bath if you wanted one. Lastly, for the more discerning and privacy-minded customer, $2.50 would secure them one of the two hundred most luxurious rooms, each of which came with its own private bathroom and toilet facilities.

(Luxury, it must be said, was a relative term when it came to the Cecil).

For a time, the hotel prospered, but gradually, its luck began to change for the worse. As happened with so many other American hotels which had been built in close proximity to the railroad, the rise of the automobile proved to be a double-edged sword. On the one hand, those citizens who could afford a car of their own had gained a degree of autonomy that allowed them to travel further afield and explore new places. On the other, the number of passengers taking the train slowly began to decline, which in turn meant that fewer people need a place to sleep when traveling across the country.

Then came the Great Depression.

Following the stock market crash of 1929, entire fortunes were wiped out almost overnight. Life savings, livelihoods, and even lives were all lost. Suicidal businessmen began jumping to their deaths from their office windows, having suddenly gone from riches to rags and seeing no option but to end it all in a final, lemming-like leap.

A massive drought known as the Dust Bowl only served to make matters worse. Now farmers felt the same pain as the financiers, and soon, so did practically every other working American. Low-income housing for families had always been a necessity in Los Angeles, and much of it surrounded the Hotel Cecil. An area of approximately fifty blocks, of which 640 Main Street became a part, came to be known by the now-familiar name of Skid Row.

One consequence of the Great Depression and the massive loss of jobs that it caused, was the willingness of working men to pack up what little they owned and travel west in search of fresh employment opportunities. For them, Los Angeles was the end of the line. Jobs were scarce, and the scant few that were available did not pay well. Skid Row was where you ended up when you had no other options and precious little hope.

Contrary to popular belief, at its inception in the 19th

century, Skid Row wasn't necessarily a bad place to be. There was land to be farmed, a few factory and construction jobs to be done. The men who worked these jobs needed somewhere affordable to live, eat, and drink. Bars, taverns, churches, and missions all rose to meet their needs. The workers sometimes even had a little money left over to go to the theater, or the music hall, if they were so inclined.

The next step down after living on Skid Row was surviving on the streets. Those who could not afford to keep a roof over their head stayed in the area, sleeping outdoors, or in one of the missions if they were lucky enough to score a bed for the night. In addition to homelessness and poverty, there were also chronic issues with alcohol, drug addiction, and mental illness among the street populace. Those on the fringes of society formed their own community on Skid Row, sometimes looking out for one another, sometimes preying on one another, depending upon desperation and circumstance. Street crime was rampant, and drug use was rife.

Churches and charities did what they could, but the term Skid Row had become synonymous with despair and desperation in the American public consciousness. Those who lived there were marginalized and avoided by the mainstream of society. As the 20th century entered its second half, few of those who came to stay at the Cecil were wealthy, or even halfway solvent. Many simply eked out what living they could, doing whatever was necessary to survive from one day to the next.

When most of the employers that had set up in Skid Row moved out, many of those who had relied upon them for survival stayed behind and became destitute.

As the Vietnam War began to wind down in the 1970s, soldiers with P.T.S.D. and drug habits gravitated into the area. It was possible to rent a cheap room at the Cecil on a weekly, or even a monthly basis. Some even made it their permanent residence, finding it more affordable than any other option they could think of.

Throughout the 1970s and 1980s, the drug problem on Skid Row (and throughout American society at large) only grew worse. Beginning in the late 1960s, a government-sanctioned push to release those diagnosed with mental illness from clinical institutions and deposit them back into the community at large led to a fresh influx of people onto the streets of Los Angeles.

The L.A.P.D. was overstretched, burdened with trying to combat open gang warfare on the streets of the city. Skid

Row was known as a high crime area, and a police response into the area was often delayed. A constant stream of drug overdoses and physical injuries kept the paramedic crews busy, with ambulances coming and going at all hours of the day and night. There was also no shortage of blazes to keep the fire department occupied.

One would think that in the 21st century, the United States, one of the world's wealthiest countries, a scientific and industrial powerhouse, would no longer have a need for somewhere like Skid Row. Sadly, in the early 2000s, things had reached what seemed to be a new low. Tent cities had sprung up along the sidewalks. Those who did not possess a tent slept in cardboard boxes, lean-to shelters, or even out in the open. The same sidewalks were used as toilets, covered in days-old human fecal matter, buzzing with flies. Small wonder that disease was rife. Doorways smelled of stale urine. Many people thought nothing of dropping their pants and relieving themselves in the street, often in plain sight of everybody else. The social niceties the rest of us take for granted don't mean much to those who are outcasts and destitute.

The drug problem had gotten worse. Narcotics, sedatives, stimulants, and countless other drugs of abuse were sold and traded openly on Skid Row. The police could barely make a dent in the illicit pharmaceutical market. Used syringes and needles littered the streets, and were washed down into the storm drains whenever it rained heavily. One didn't have to look far in order to find a smashed crack pipe, bong, or other drug paraphernalia that had been abandoned by its user.

Today, Skid Row is still a forlorn place. Many of the homeless occupants are increasingly vulnerable because of their advanced age (many are older than 65) and the ever-present problems with drugs and crime are far from gone.

Still, there is some reason for hope. Not every occupant of Skid Row lives on the street, and it's important to make it clear that many, if not most of them are not criminals. A significant number of them still call residential hotels their home. Some are retirees, getting by on a limited income. Others are recovered or recovering addicts, brave souls who have somehow beaten the odds and are working hard to rebuild lives that were damaged and broken by addiction.

There are also initiatives underway to provide housing for those who currently have none. One option that is no longer open to those seeking a place to live is the Hotel Cecil, whose doors closed to the public on January 1, 2017.

In 2013, attempts were made to turn almost four hundred

of the hotel's vacant rooms into affordable living space for the homeless population. Politicians and business owners in the area vociferously opposed the plan, which never came to fruition. Had it been successful, one must wonder just how many homeless people would have gotten an opportunity to make a fresh start and get off the streets of Skid Row.

Instead, the Cecil became a place of myth. One legend with some truth to it maintains that so many guests took their lives there down through the years, that the Cecil eventually acquired the nickname "the Suicide."

In close to one hundred years, the guest rooms of the Hotel Cecil have seen the highs and lows of human experience, and everything in between.

Love.

Hate.

Hope.

Fear.

Joy.

Sorrow.

The entire gamut of emotions has been run within those walls.

If only they could talk.

CHAPTER TWO
Unattended Death

It is an unavoidable fact of life that people die in hotels and motels all the time. I can attest to this from personal experience. As a paramedic, I have worked cardiac arrests in hotels on multiple occasions. Sometimes, the decedent passes away quietly, dying in their sleep of natural causes; on other occasions, drugs or violence play a role. Sometimes both.

Several years ago, I was working as a part-time adjunct instructor at a paramedic academy. The senior instructor was a highly respected and innovative educator, and he loved to get the students out of the classroom whenever the opportunity presented itself.

On this particular morning, I was slowly working my way through rush hour traffic when my phone rang. "Change of plan today," he told me. "Don't come to class. Go to this address instead."

The address he gave me was that of a motel. When I saw the name, I knew that this was not a nice place. My suspicions were confirmed when I pulled up in the parking lot and headed to the room whose number he had given me.

As soon as the instructor opened the door and I stepped inside the room, my nose wrinkled in disgust. The carpet was threadbare, and the place obviously hadn't been decorated since the 1970s or 1980s at the very latest. Paint was peeling from the walls. Inside the bathroom, a layer of rust and scum encircled the shower drain and bathtub. It was the kind of place where you wanted to wipe your feet on the way out, and was barely one step up from the sort of motel where you rented the rooms by the half hour.

That wasn't why I wrinkled my nose, though. It was the smell. A musty, vaguely unsettling odor permeated everything. I just assumed it was part of the motel's timeless charm and tried to tune it out. We brought in a training ambulance staffed by student paramedics and gave them a simulated patient encounter in the room, using an instructor to play the role of a combative, belligerent resident who would ultimately turn out to have a low blood sugar.

The morning went by fast. At noon, we all went to get lunch. When we came back, I was surprised to see two police cruisers parked outside our door. "Which room are you in?" one of the officers asked. I pointed, wondering what we'd done wrong. Had there been a noise complaint? Our training exercise *had* gotten a little rowdy, but I didn't think we'd been *that* bad.

"What's going on?" I asked the cop. He pointed toward the room next to ours with his thumb.

"Dead guy." His bored tone of voice and casual manner suggested that this was a thing which happened all the time at this motel.

I should have been surprised, but then the reason for the smell dawned on me. The door to that room was open just a crack. As I walked toward our room, I couldn't resist a quick look. The dead man was face down with his buttocks in the air, as naked as the day he'd been born. I could see a few tattoos, but that was it. There didn't seem to be a mark on him. Based on the stiffness and angle of the dead man's limbs, it looked as though rigor mortis had already set in. His lower hemisphere was almost completely purple, where the blood had pooled after his heart stopped beating.

We did what all paramedics would do in a situation like that: we went back to work. I never did find out whether foul play or drugs were involved, whether it was "just his time," or if there was anything more to the story. The police officer's demeanor made it very clear that this particular motel was known for its guests turning up dead.

To this day, whenever I drive past that place, I get a mental flashback to the guy lying dead on the stained and dirty carpet. To be honest, it creeps me out a little that once the body was taken away by the coroner, the room would have gotten at best a quick steam clean and vacuum before the next tenant was allowed to take up residence. No mention of the death would ever be made. It makes me wonder how many times I've checked into a hotel room in which someone has recently died, and I've known absolutely nothing about it.

Quite understandably, hotel owners and managers don't like to talk about these things, let alone publicize them. It's considered poor form to spook the guests, not to mention being bad for business. The British comedy actor John Cleese, best known for his work as part of the *Monty Python* comedy troupe, once reminisced about his greatest television creation, the hotelier Basil Fawlty, in the classic sitcom *Fawlty Towers*. Cleese had been inspired to create the character of Fawlty after he and his fellow Pythons stayed in a hotel run by a particularly eccentric manager. In the episode *The Kipper and The Corpse*, Basil and his staff are caught in a tricky situation after one of the guests is found to have passed away. Cleese explained during an interview that the idea for this episode originated with a conversation he once had with the manager of London's prestigious Savoy Hotel. When Cleese asked what the most difficult thing about running such a hotel was, the manager replied that it was dealing discreetly with all of the dead guests!

The point I'm trying to make here is that hotel deaths happen, and they happen often. The busier a hotel is, the more people that pass through its doors on a yearly basis, the greater the likelihood that a handful of them will die before getting the opportunity to check out. Heart attacks and cardiac arrests do occur, and they are no great respecter of whether their victim is laying in their own bed or that of an unsuspecting hotelier. It is far from unusual for somebody to pass away in their room, only to be discovered the following morning by a member of the cleaning staff coming in to change the linens.

It's also a sad truth that each year, a sizeable number of people check into hotels with the express purpose of ending their own lives. The reasons for this are many. Sometimes, it's a desire to take one's own life away from the presence of friends and family. People have been known to travel long distances, sometimes even journeying to other countries, in order to do this. The act of physically separating oneself from one's loved ones and associates can sometimes make a difficult act a little easier to carry out.

One such case hits very close to home.

The year was 1997. A 54-year-old woman named Kari Miller, who came from Englewood, Colorado, bought a one-way ticket from Denver to Michigan, where she drove to Roseville and checked into a motel. She had an appointment to keep. The man she was due to meet arrived three hours late, and intentionally so. Rather than being tardy, he had wanted to give her one last chance to change her mind.

She did not.

The man was Dr. Jack Kevorkian, and the woman was my wife's mother. (My wife has given permission for me to share this story). Like far too many Coloradoans, she had been diagnosed with Multiple Sclerosis, a progressively degenerative disease which afflicts a disproportionate number of those who live in and around this part of the Rocky Mountains.

Before making what would turn out to be her final appointment with a doctor, Kari Miller had written a letter explaining her reasons for seeking to end her own life. She mailed the letter to her own physician prior to her death.

The pain I was forced to live with and what MS had done to me became intolerable. I no longer chose to live my life suffering with the constant pain of being so disabled.

Many of the approximately 130 patients Jack Kevorkian assisted in taking their own lives were MS sufferers, and several of them met the doctor in a hotel or motel room. Their bodies were usually found either later that night or early the following day, often accompanied by a note listing the phone number of Kevorkian's lawyer along with a request that he be called.

One cannot help but feel sympathy for the hotel staff who entered the room and discovered the body, even if (as was sometimes the case) they had some forewarning of what awaited them. My mother in law's assisted death went about as smoothly as such a momentous event could, by all accounts. Most of those who take their own lives in hotel rooms do not have access to a physician willing to help them die, and so the methods open to them are cruder and far less clinical. Incurable medical conditions are an understandable reason for a human being to reach such a level of despair that suicide may seem like the only way out.

An unspecified illness caused 55-year-old Louis D. Borden to take his own life on July 26, 1934. Born in Salina, Kansas, Borden had been a sergeant in the U.S. Army Medical Corps, but he was a civilian when he checked into the Hotel

Cecil. It would be reasonable to assume that with a medical background, he would have possessed a working knowledge of drugs and pharmaceuticals, but if so, Mr. Borden did not choose to take a fatal overdose of painkillers or any other medication in order to make his exit from the world. Instead, the former military man took a straight razor and drew it across his throat. The neck is very vascular, and neither the jugular veins or carotid arteries are particularly deep or well-protected by the connective tissue and skin.

Slicing one's own throat takes courage. It is a very bloody and undignified way to die, particularly when one or more of the major blood vessels are severed – which is the intent behind doing it. Arterial spray can project out several feet from the self-inflicted wound. One small mercy is that due to the sheer speed of the blood loss, the victim loses consciousness rapidly and usually does not regain it. Louis Borden's body was found with the razor laying close by, accompanied by letters explaining several reasons for his death. Only one such reason was listed in the newspaper: that Mr. Borden was experiencing "some kind of problem with his health."

Sergeant Borden's death was officially listed as a suicide, which it most likely was, and his reason for taking his own life — illness — makes complete sense. There's no reason to suspect foul play. But was he experiencing difficulties in his personal life as well? According to the *Los Angeles Times*, Louis Borden left a message bequeathing his possessions to "Mrs. Edna Hasoner of PO Box 664, Edmonds, Wash., sole beneficiary of the little I leave." Mrs. Hasoner was not, however, Louis Borden's wife. According to his entry on the website *www.findagrave.com* (which was created by the U.S. Veterans Affairs Office) the former sergeant's spouse was one Margaret Rachel McLeod. Their year of marriage is listed as 1912.

Who, then, was Mrs. Edna Hasoner? Were Louis and Margaret separated, or estranged? Had Edna become Louis's new flame, or was she just a treasured friend? Perhaps she was their daughter, or a sister, and Hasoner was her married name. She was obviously a significant part of his life, or why else would he have made her the beneficiary of his few remaining earthly possessions?

Louis Borden is buried in the Los Angeles National Cemetery, with a headstone which appropriately depicts his military service. Considering the tragic circumstances surrounding his death, we can only hope that the sergeant now rests peacefully.

[FORMER SOLDIER TAKES HIS OWN LIFE, Los Angeles Times, 27 July, 1934]

It can sometimes be a red flag if the guest who is checking into a hotel happens to live locally. The rationale here is straightforward: if you have a home in the vicinity, there are few reasons for you to spend the night in a hotel. An illicit love affair, perhaps, or an argument with a significant other. Sometimes, abuse of some form has taken place. Hotel managers and those staff members who work the reception desk are often taught to watch out for such things. However, not all of them are willing to ask too many questions.

On Saturday, September 17, 1932, a gunshot rang out inside the walls of the Hotel Cecil. When cleaning maid Mrs. Carrie Brown went into the room, she found the body of 25-year-old Benjamin Dodich sprawled in a pool of his own blood. Mr. Dodich had been killed by a single gunshot wound to the head, piercing his right temple and inflicting catastrophic injury to the brain. The dead man lived just two miles away from the hotel, and he had checked into the Cecil only a few hours before his corpse was discovered.

Homicide detectives came to the scene and investigated his death. They found no apparent motive for the young man to have taken his own life, or for somebody else to have murdered him. While it has long been presumed a suicide, the case has never been satisfactorily explained, and it's likely that it never will be.

CHAPTER THREE
Poison

Drug overdoses are a common method of taking one's own life, be it with illicit street drugs or prescription medications. Pills are often washed down with alcohol, not only as a means of making the ingestion easier, but also as a way of getting up the courage to actually go through with taking them in the first place.

Taking poison is also a frequently chosen option.

It was Saturday, November 14, 1931, when James Willys, a 46-year-old man who claimed to hail from Chicago, entered the opulent lobby of the Hotel Cecil and walked up to the front desk. He asked for a room, signed himself in, paid, and was given a key. As far as we know, the staff member who served Mr. Willys noticed nothing particularly unusual about him at the time. They certainly had no reason to suspect that James Willys of Chicago was actually nothing of the sort.

His real name was W.K. Norton, and he lived much closer than the Windy City —he had a place in Manhattan Beach, just fifteen miles away. Norton had disappeared from his home earlier that Saturday, and his whereabouts would remain unknown until his dead body was discovered by a maid inside his room at the Hotel Cecil.

The police were duly called. The dead man's room was searched, and so was his body. Frisking his clothes, the officers found several capsules in the pockets of his vest. These pills turned out to be poison, and were believed to have been the cause of his death. There were also checks, made payable to a Mrs. M.C. Norton, which allowed the police to establish the identity of the deceased.

[*SEARCH FOR MAN ENDS IN FINDING BODY AT HOTEL*, Los Angeles Times, 19 November 1931]

W.K. Norton may have been the Hotel Cecil's first poisoning death (on record, at least), but he wouldn't be the last. Several years later, on 28 May, 1939, a U.S. Navy sailor named Erwin C. Neblett imbibed a lethal dose of strychnine while staying there. The Radioman 2nd Class was assigned to the *USS Wright*, a seaplane tender which was berthed in San Diego. Mr. Neblett's reasons for taking his own life are unknown.

Mr. Neblett was found sprawled on the floor of his hotel room, unconscious but still alive, by a maid entering the room to clean it. A letter addressed to his uncle, one Dr. Douglas Neblett of Staten Island, New York, was found alongside his body. Its contents remain a mystery, although we can reasonably infer that it would have been a suicide note.

Yet again, the L.A.P.D. was called to the Cecil, but by the time they arrived, the unfortunate sailor was beyond saving. There are some disputes as to his age, with some sources claiming that he was 34 years old, and others stating his age as 39. After being carefully prepared by morticians, Erwin Neblett's body was returned to his native Clarksville, Tennessee for burial.

The unopened letter had been given to employees of the Long Beach-based mortuary which had taken care of his remains prior to shipping them home. Despite the *Los Angeles Times* stating that Erwin Neblett had died at the Cecil, his local newspaper, the *Clarksville Leaf-Chronicle,* reported that he had died while staying at his naval base "after a brief illness." With his funeral set for Sunday, 4 June, the version printed in the Leaf-Chronicle listed his cause of death as an unexpected heart attack. Of poisoning or suicide, there was no mention, perhaps as a kindness to his family.

Strychnine is a pesticide, most often used for killing rats and other rodents. When ingested in lethal quantities, strychnine poisoning can be an extremely painful and unpleasant way to die. It interferes with the signals that enervate the muscles, making it difficult or impossible for the body to switch them off.

Depending on how concentrated the strychnine happens to be, and also upon the amount ingested, the first symptoms of poisoning can onset within a quarter of an hour after the substance first enters the body. The result is a series of muscular fasciculations, spastic twitching, and finally, full-body convulsions akin to those of a tonic-clonic seizure. The respiratory muscles, which are responsible for keeping the human body breathing, suffer violent spasms, until finally the person stops breathing. It then takes just seconds for the patient to transition from respiratory arrest into cardiac arrest.

We can only hope that Erwin Neblett did not suffer too greatly. It is not unusual for those who are poisoned with strychnine to remain conscious until they are quite close to the end of life.

The tragic story of Erwin Neblett's death ends with an equally sad coda. His father, Lewis, was a doctor in Clarksville. By all accounts, he was a much liked and popular member of the community. He also had a strong work ethic, still practicing medicine at the age of 73. At around six o'clock in the evening on December 25, 1939 — Christmas Night — almost seven months after the death of his son, Dr. Neblett made a house call on one of his patients. Feeling fatigued, he then went home and lay down to rest before dinner.

He never woke up.

The *Leaf-Chronicle* reported:

Dr. Neblett had not been well for six weeks. Worry over the unexpected death of his son, Erwin, in California last May, and about his home being seriously damaged by fire a short time ago, is believed to have hastened his death. [*DR. NEBLETT, 73, DIES SUDDENLY AT HOME HERE,* Clarksville Leaf-Chronicle, 26 December, 1939]

It would appear that the events which took place in Erwin Neblett's room at the Hotel Cecil would have equally tragic consequences further down the line. Dr. Lewis Neblett is buried in the Greenwood Cemetery, Clarksville, in plot 2 — the same plot in which Erwin's grave can also be found.

[*SAILOR ENDS LIFE BY TAKING POISON,* Los Angeles Times, 29 May, 1939]

[*SAILOR KILLS SELF,* Daily News, 29 May, 1939]

[*SAILOR SUICIDES*, Nevada State Journal, 29 May, 1939]

[NEBLETT DIES IN SAN DIEGO: CLARKSVILLE BOY'S BODY TO BE RETURNED HERE FOR BURIAL, Clarksville Leaf-Chronicle, 29 May, 1939]

[NEBLETT'S RITES TO BE SUNDAY: BODY LEFT SAN DIEGO THURSDAY AFTERNOON — DIED OF HEART ATTACK, Clarksville Leaf-Chronicle, 4 June, 1939]

The following year, another suicide by poisoning was attempted at the Cecil. 45-year-old Dorothy Seger from Riverside, a teacher by profession, took an unidentified poison while in her room. The *Los Angeles Times* reported her condition as "near death" at the city's Receiving Hospital, in its 11 January, 1940 edition. She died the following day, on 12 January. The reasons for taking her own life remain a mystery, one that is unlikely to ever be solved.

One thing can be said about her state of mind, however: Dorothy's actions were almost certainly premeditated. She checked into the Cecil under the name of Evelyn Brent, and after settling in, wrote to her family and gave them advanced notice that she intended to kill herself. Although she did not die at the Hotel Cecil, the actions which ultimately led to Dorothy Seger's death did take place there.

[*TEACHER NEAR DEATH,* The Los Angeles Times, 11 January, 1940]

[GIRL ATTEMPTS DEATH WHEN DENIED MOVIE; 3 KILL SELVES, the Los Angeles Times, 13 January, 1940]

As a young, newly trained Emergency Medical Technician, I once responded to a hotel for a man believed to be dead, and unwittingly had my own brush with death by poison. We were told by dispatch that the cleaner opened the door to his room and was shocked to see its resident lying naked and face down on the floor. Horrified, she immediately left the room, closing the door behind her, and called 911.

My ambulance arrived at the same time as the fire engine. My paramedic partner and I went inside along with the firefighters. My partner took a knee, checking to see whether the patient had a pulse, but the patient's color was such that we could all tell he had been dead for a while.

"Hey," one of the firefighters said, sniffing at the air. "Do you smell that?"

He was right. There was a strange smell, hard to describe, but something like wood smoke — an odd thing to smell in a hotel room that was right in the heart of a major city.

I was distracted by the cardiac monitor, but luckily the firefighters were a little more observant than me. "There's something written on the bathroom door," he said.

We all looked up. The bathroom door was halfway open. Taped to the front of it was a sign, scrawled in black permanent marker.

DANGER! — POISON!

"Get out! Now!" the fire lieutenant said. There's an unwritten rule that nobody runs on an emergency scene. We broke it without thinking twice, heading straight for the door and slamming it behind us.

What followed was a long and excruciating wait for the Haz-mat team to assemble and make entry to the room, in order to figure out what the poison was. Some kind of unidentified gas seemed reasonable, based on what we'd smelled. Whatever it was, we'd all been exposed. Our vital signs were all normal (with the exception of a racing heartbeat in a couple of cases) but it was hard to not worry about having breathed in something toxic.

In the end, it turned out to be something that was,

paradoxically, both lethal and relatively benign at the same time. In the bathroom, the Haz-mat technicians found a big stack of charcoal briquettes, of the type commonly used to fuel a barbecue. The hotel guest had closed himself in the bathroom, set light to the charcoal, and waited in the tub. For as long as the briquettes burned, they emitted carbon monoxide, a colorless, odorless, and tasteless gas that is highly toxic. What we were smelling was a lingering odor of charcoal residue.

As the levels of carbon monoxide built up in the man's bloodstream, it displaced the oxygen from his hemoglobin. He began to get drowsy. Finally, the gas reached toxic levels. It is likely that, as long as well-meaning rescuers hadn't interrupted him, he would have simply slipped away into death. Sometimes, this can be a peaceful way to die. Unfortunately, this wasn't one of those times. As best we could tell, as the gas began to affect his brain, the man suffered an episode of altered mental status and panicked, getting out of the bathtub, throwing open the bathroom door, and collapsing face down on the carpet in front of it. That is where he died, and where we eventually found him.

Carbon monoxide has long been used as a method of committing suicide, most often by affixing a rubber hose to the tailpipe of a running vehicle and feeding the opposite end in through the window. Alternatively, running a car in a garage for a prolonged period of time can also prove to be fatal. Charcoal-burning suicide occurs when somebody burns fuel inside an enclosed space, allowing carbon monoxide to slowly reach toxic levels. This has happened inside camper vans, tents, storage units...and hotel rooms.

Not everybody who commits suicide in a hotel takes poison. Some go with more violent methods, such as cutting their wrists, usually in a bathtub full of water, or shooting themselves. These death scenes are nothing less than horrific, and can also be extremely traumatizing for the unfortunate employee who stumbles upon them.

Money can't buy happiness, as the old saying goes, but it certainly can help. At least, it certainly helps *some* people, but by no means all. This sad truth was borne out on January 22, 1927, when a 52-year-old Providence, Rhode Island man named Percy Ormond Cook spent his last hours on Earth as a guest at the Hotel Cecil.

The owner of an apartment complex, with a respectable

and lucrative career in real estate, Cook had been successful by most definitions of the word, but the external veneer was far from the true story. In the months leading up to this day, he had been estranged from both his wife and his son. The Christmas and New Year holiday season had come and gone, always a bad time to be alone, made even worse by being separated from his family.

Lonely and growing increasingly desperate, Percy Cook had sunk into a downward spiral of depression and despair from which there was no escape. Finally, he decided that there was no other choice than to end it all. Writing first to the wife from whom he was now living apart, Percy told her that he was going to kill himself.

The hours passed. Then days. There was no response to his letter, no heartfelt plea for reconciliation. Percy tried to summon up the courage to end his own life, but always stopped short of actually doing it. We can only imagine how cold and lonely his room at the Cecil must have felt. It took him a week, but finally, he sat down with a sheet of paper and wrote out a message for those who would soon find his body.

Money cannot buy happiness. I have tried it and I find that it cannot be done. I have lost my wife, my son, and my home, and I am doing the only thing left for me to do.

In the preceding months, Percy Cook claimed to have spent $40,000 (close to $600,000 in 2021 money) in the pursuit of happiness. It was all to no avail. Finally, unable to bear the misery and the loneliness any longer, he took a gun, loaded it, and shot himself inside his hotel room.

The gunshot was not immediately fatal. Percy was rushed to the closest medical facility, the Receiving Hospital, where doctors examined him and pronounced him likely to die. Their prognosis was correct. Percy Ormond Cook died later that day, secondary to trauma inflicted by the gunshot wound. His body was sent back to Providence, and he was buried in the Swan Point Cemetery.

[*MARITAL STRIFE HELD CAUSE OF SUICIDE ATTEMPT,* Los Angeles Times, 23 Jan, 1927]

CHAPTER FOUR
Fallen

We can only imagine how terrifying it must feel to fall to one's death. Seeing the ground rising up to meet you, knowing that it's impossible to turn back the clock and change things. Does your life *really* flash before your eyes in those final few seconds, everything from birth to death, every significant moment, whether good or bad, replayed in the blink of an eye that somehow seems to last for an eternity?

The Cecil has unfortunately had more than its fair share of residents fall to their deaths from an upper floor. Indeed, it is by far the most common cause of death associated with the hotel. Some may have slipped accidentally. Others jumped intentionally. As we will soon see, in one particularly horrific instance, at least one of them was thrown out of a window.

On March 14, 1937, 26-year-old Grace Magro fell from the Hotel Cecil's ninth floor. Her body plunged through some telephone wires on the way down, which slowed her fall just enough to save her life. This may seem like a blessing, but the truth is that the poor young woman would have suffered horribly after hitting the ground from nine stories up. When police officers arrived on scene, they found Grace's broken body wrapped up in the vestiges of those same wires.

She was taken to the Los Angeles Receiving Hospital for treatment, but there was simply no way even such a young woman could survive multi-systems trauma of that magnitude, and she subsequently died of her injuries.

Police officers investigated the circumstances surrounding Grace Magro's death, trying to determine whether she had deliberately jumped, had somehow slipped and fallen from an open window, or whether she might have been pushed. Grace had been sharing her room with a man named M.W. Madison, who was a sailor assigned to the *USS Virginia*. It is not known where Grace's husband, Willard, was at the time, or whether the two were even still together.

At any rate, Madison insisted that he had been asleep at the time Grace plunged from the ninth floor, and according to the *Los Angeles Times*, "J. B. Read., Jr, manager of the hotel, corroborated his story." One is forced to wonder exactly how the hotel's manager could swear that one of his guests had been sleeping at the exact moment his companion died. Without having been in the guests' room himself at the time, how could he possibly have known? Still, the police seem to have accepted their stories, because no charges were ever filed.

Grace Magro was laid to rest in the Odd Fellows Cemetery, located in the Boyle Heights district of L.A. The cemetery made national news during the 1980s when 16,433 aborted fetuses were buried there after they had been discovered in a storage container rented by the owner of a medical laboratory. The ensuing national scandal and subsequent litigation went all the way to the Supreme Court, and the case received a great deal of attention from then-president Ronald Reagan.

On January 9, 1938, marine fireman Roy Thompson climbed to the fourteenth floor of the Cecil and jumped — or so it is assumed. No witnesses came forward to confirm what had happened, but foul play was never declared. Mr. Thompson's body struck the roof of a nearby building, where it landed on top of a skylight, according to the *Wilmington Daily Press Journal*. [*FIREMAN ON SHIP IN SUICIDE LEAP,* January 10, 1938]

Almost a decade passed without a guest jumping to their death. Then, in October of 1947, 35-year-old Robert Smith suffered a fatal fall from half the building's height, seven stories up.

[*BODY IDENTIFIED IN HOTEL ROOM FALL*, Los Angeles Times, 1 November, 1947]

What was it about the hotel's seventh floor which made it such a magnet for jumpers? Seven years later, on October 22, 1954, 55-year-old stationery worker Helen C. Gurnee chose to end her life by jumping from the window of Room #704. It was one week after she had first arrived in downtown L.A. Just like others who died at the Cecil over the years, Ms. Gurnee had checked in at the hotel's front desk using an alias: she claimed to be one Margaret Brown of Denver. Readers with a knowledge of history will instantly make the connection with the real-life legend Margaret "the Unsinkable Molly" Brown, famed socialite and survivor of the *RMS Titanic* disaster. Margaret Brown had indeed lived in Denver — in fact, her house is still there, is now a museum, and regularly attracts visitors who are eager to learn more about the pioneering Mrs. Brown. I can also attest from personal experience that the Molly Brown House has ghosts of its own.

The real Margaret Brown died in 1932, some twenty-two years before her namesake fell to her death from the Hotel Cecil's seventh floor. She landed on the hotel's marquee, which was more than sufficient to draw a large crowd of gawking passers-by. The public milled around and watched as a fire engine arrived and laddered the marquee so that the dead woman's body could be retrieved and taken away.

Once again, the reasons behind Helen Gurnee's suicide are opaque to us. She spent a week living at the Cecil, perhaps mulling over her options, before taking the very final path upon which she ultimately embarked.

[*WOMAN KILLED IN SEVEN-FLOOR HOTEL PLUNGE,* Los Angeles Times, 23 October 1954].

In the early morning hours of Sunday, 11 February, 1962, 47-year-old Julia Frances Sloan Moore jumped from the Cecil's eighth floor. Rather than hitting the ground, her body hit the second floor roof. She had checked in at the Cecil on Wednesday the 7th. Julia left no suicide note behind to explain her last actions.

When L.A.P.D. officers searched her room, they found a purse and a bag with clothes and toiletries, plus fifty-nine cents in cash — the equivalent of about $4.60 at 2021 rates. Yet she was far from broke, having a bank book with $1800 among her possessions — approximately $15,600 in today's money. The cash was deposited in a bank located in Springfield, Illinois. A bus ticket stub suggested that Julia had traveled to Los Angeles from St. Louis, although little is known of her life or motives. It is believed that she was born in Arkansas on 9 October, 1914, and she is also buried there. Why she made the long journey west and then ended her own life, we will probably never know.

[*WOMAN LEAPS TO DEATH FROM HOTEL WINDOW*, Los Angeles Times, 12 February, 1962].

Later that year, on Saturday, 12 October, 1962, another suicide by jumping incident made headlines because it involved not one but rather two deaths. Ask any police officer, and they'll tell you that domestic quarrels and disputes can escalate quickly and get out of hand. Such was the case with 27-year-old Pauline Otton, who was staying at the Cecil with her husband. The two were estranged, and had checked into the hotel earlier that day. Mr. Otton would later say that Pauline had visited him at his place of work, where she had floated the idea of possibly getting back together.

It is impossible to say exactly what transpired in their ninth-floor hotel room, but Mr. Otton told police officers that he had left Pauline alone in order to go out and get something to eat. After he was gone, she somehow fell from the window and plunged all nine stories to the sidewalk below, where an unsuspecting gentleman named George

Gianinni happened to be walking. Pauline Otton landed right on top of him, killing him outright.

Detectives were puzzled at first, initially thinking that a double jumping had taken place. It soon became apparent that this was not the case, because the body of George Gianinni still wore shoes, which would have been thrown clear if he had hit the ground after a nine-story fall. Supporting the theory that the 65-year-old man had just been taking a stroll was the fact that the dead man's hands were found to be in his trouser pockets, an incredibly unlikely thing to happen to a falling body. They finally decided that the unfortunate man had simply been in the wrong place at the wrong time, a piece of grim misfortune that had cost him his life.

The story was considered macabre enough to be carried over the various wire services, such as the Associated Press (AP) and United Press International (UPI) and made news across America.

[*SUICIDE'S PLUNGING BODY STRIKES, KILLS PASSERBY IN LA*, The Sacramento Bee, 13 October, 1962]

[*NINE FLOOR PLUNGE: WOMAN'S DEATH LEAP KILLS MAN ON STREET*, Los Angeles Times, 13 October, 1962]

On December 16, 1975, at 12:05pm, a young woman registered at the Cecil under the name Alison Lowell. Afterward, when police officers launched an investigation, they were unable to track down anybody by that name. Ms. Lowell was given the key to Room #327.

Four days later, on December 20, she took the 10-story fall from the twelfth floor down to the second-floor roof. So great was the blunt force trauma inflicted on her body that her facial features were damaged beyond all recognition. Exactly how and why she came to fall remains as much a mystery as her identity still does. What we *do* know is that she was Caucasian, with brown hair, brown eyes, and was believed to have been in her twenties at the time of her death.

The only distinguishing features were scars on both of her wrists. One of the few clues to her place of origin was a ticket stub issued by the Greyhound Bus company, with a starting point of Bakersfield, California, that was found in her hotel room. The ticket had been purchased on December 15, the day before she had checked in to the Cecil.

It is saddening to think that somewhere, "Alison Lowell" may still have family members who miss her, loved ones who still agonize over what happened to their mother, daughter, sister, or niece. Unfortunately, more than forty-five years after her death, the chance that this particular Jane Doe will ever be identified, remain slim, and continue to shrink with each passing year.

[https://mec.lacounty.gov/unidentified-person-detail/?caseNumber=1975-15414]

[http://www.doenetwork.org/cases/1365ufca.html]

Records show that the hotel had a seventeen-year respite from deaths by jumping. On 1 September, 1992, a little before one o'clock in the morning, the body of an African-American man in his twenties was discovered in an alleyway behind the Cecil. The young man had dark hair, brown eyes, and scarring on the back of his right hand. He wore a T-shirt bearing the logo: *New York. Fun times. Good times.*

It is believed that this particular John Doe had fallen from the roof, although police investigators cannot state definitively whether he slipped and fell, jumped intentionally, or was pushed.

Despite the unfortunate man's face being sufficiently intact that an artist was able to draw it, nobody has yet come forward to identify him.

[https://mec.lacounty.gov/unidentified-person-detail/?caseNumber=1992-08017]

[http://www.doenetwork.org/cases/707umca.html]

The Cecil's final jumping death, at the time of writing (and hopefully, forever) took place on Friday June 12, 2015. The body of a young man was found on the street outside the hotel, shortly before five o'clock in the afternoon. He appeared to have fallen from a great height. Paramedics pronounced the 28-year-old dead at the scene. Hotel management told reporters that the dead man was not a hotel guest, then added that did not know who he was. Police were able to identify him, but they did not release the name to the media at the time.

Hopefully, this unfortunate man will close the book for good on the subject of death at the Hotel Cecil.

[DEATH OUTSIDE SKID ROW HOTEL IS INVESTIGATED AS POSSIBLE SUICIDE, THE LOS ANGELES TIMES, 13 June, 2015]

CHAPTER FIVE
The Killings

Despite its having been given the nickname of "the Suicide," due to the number of guests who took their own lives during their stay, the Hotel Cecil was also the scene of two killings. I say "killings" rather than murders because of the first case, that of Dorothy Jean Purcell and her newborn baby son.

The year was 1944. By that summer, Allied forces had landed on the continent of Europe and begun the liberation of France from Nazi occupation. Many of those soldiers, sailors, airmen and marines were American, and together they formed the mightiest military machine ever assembled.

On the home front, the engines of industry were humming. Supporting the military was big business, and 19-year-old Dorothy Jean Purcell had left her home and family behind in Iowa, to travel west in search of work in the defense sector. After arriving on the West Coast, she had reconnected with a man named Anthony Carther. Purcell claimed to have been acquainted with Carther from her Iowa days, and when later questioned by police, said that he was the father of her child.

It was late August when a heavily pregnant Dorothy Purcell checked into the Hotel Cecil. Accompanying her was a man twice her age, 38-year-old shoe salesman Ben Levine. Perhaps in order to stave off any potential scandal, Purcell and Levine were posing as a married couple on their arrival. Or perhaps, giving him the benefit of the doubt, Mr. Levine was simply being gentlemanly, assisting a young, unmarried mother through the final stages of her pregnancy discreetly.

Early in the morning on Sunday, 3 September, Dorothy began to experience labor pains. In all likelihood, they woke her up. Rather than seek medical attention, or even wake her companion, she instead went to the washroom and delivered the baby herself. To give birth alone, in a strange place far from home, is a sad and frightening thing. We can only imagine what was going through the young woman's mind as she groaned and grunted her way through the birthing process.

Once the delivery was complete, Dorothy must have somehow tied off the umbilical cord and cut it. By her own account, she then stood looking at the face of her newborn son. His eyes were closed, the facial features slack, his body totally flaccid.

Dorothy Purcell would say later that she believed her son had just emerged from her body stillborn. Making her way to an upper floor of the hotel, she opened a window, and threw the helpless newborn out. Then, astonishingly, she returned to her room, and acted as if nothing untoward had happened.

The baby boy weighed just five pounds. His broken, lifeless body would later be found on the roof of a building next door to the Cecil.

Police responded to the hotel, taking both Dorothy and Ben Levine into custody. A murder investigation then ensued. Dorothy's health quickly declined, due to an aggressive post-partum infection that was so serious, she needed to be hospitalized. That did not stop a coroner's jury trial taking place in her absence.

An autopsy was performed on the infant's body. The verdict: due to the state of his lungs, which had been inflated with air at the time of his death, the baby boy had definitely been born alive. His mother had gotten it tragically wrong in believing that he was stillborn. More likely, the coroner's autopsy surgeon Frank Webb would testify in court, the newborn had simply required vigorous stimulation such as a slap on the buttocks, to show signs of life.

The question was now raised: had Dorothy Purcell committed murder, or was this all simply a tragic, ghastly mistake? The coroner's jury returned a verdict of homicide, meaning that there would now need to be a murder trial.

[*MOTHER HELD AFTER BABY FOUND THROWN TO DEATH*, Los Angeles Times, 8 September 1944]

[*MOTHER FACES TRIAL FOR ROOF DEATH OF BABY,* Daily News, 8 September, 1944]

The trial took place early the following year. The jury found Dorothy guilty not of murder, but of manslaughter, with the addition of diminished responsibility — in other words, the insanity defense. Her legal counsel successfully argued that Dorothy was so emotionally traumatized, she was rendered temporarily insane at the time she threw her infant son from the heights of the Hotel Cecil.

Personally, I find it to be a very believable and persuasive argument. It would take an immensely callous, almost soulless individual to do what she had done. A psychopath or sociopath. Even taking her account at face value, and accepting that she had thought the baby to be dead at the time, the urge to hurl it out of a window makes little rational sense. Had she been a cunning, conniving young woman — and there's no evidence to suggest that she was — then there would have been countless different ways to have disposed of the infant discreetly; ways far less likely to point the finger back at her. She could have walked several blocks from the hotel and hidden the tiny body at the bottom of a trash can, or even traveled a little further afield by means of public transport, and then thrown it into the Pacific Ocean. It only stood to reason that the baby's remains would land in a public place, and that the police would comb all of the surrounding buildings for suspects. The moment an officer asked the hotel staff whether any of the Cecil's guests had a baby with them, the jig would have been up.

After giving birth all alone in a shower room, what the stunned young woman did next was appalling, shocking, and was so far removed from what any other human being would have done, that it easily met the definition of insanity.

Apparently, the jury agreed. Declared temporarily insane at the time, but with her sanity now restored, she walked out of the courtroom and disappeared from the newspapers and history books. Whether her experience at the Hotel Cecil haunted her for the remainder of her life, or whether she even remembered what had happened on that Sunday morning in Los Angeles, remains unknown.

[*IOWA GIRL FREED,* Quad-City Times (Davenport, Iowa), 7 January, 1945].

While the death of Dorothy Purcell's newborn child was

declared to not be a murder, the same most definitely cannot be said about that of "Pigeon" Goldie Osgood some twenty years later.

The 65-year-old woman was a long-term resident of the Cecil, having lived there permanently in the six year period leading up to her death. A retired telephone switchboard operator, she was a friendly, sociable woman, almost universally liked and completely inoffensive. Wearing her distinctive L.A. Dodgers baseball cap, she was a familiar sight in nearby Pershing Square, where she liked nothing better than to feed the pigeons — hence her nickname. She was very fond of the birds, and she liked to make sure that even the smallest got their fair share of the food. Sometimes that meant shooing the bigger ones out of the way so that the weaker birds could eat. That was about the limit of Goldie's aggressiveness.

Goldie Osgood was a harmless soul if ever there was one, the sort of person about whom others would say: "She hadn't an enemy in the world." Which only makes it all the more tragic that she was the victim of a savage and murderous attack.

On Thursday, 4 June, 1964, a hotel employee named Logan Kalv was distributing new copies of the phone book to the rooms at the Cecil. He found the door to Goldie's room unlocked and, presumably after knocking, went inside. There he discovered her lifeless, blood-stained body. She had been stabbed above her left breast, and a hand towel had been used to strangle her.

Goldie's Dodgers ball cap sat at her bedside. Among the few other personal possessions she had, were three 10-lb bags of bird seed. Her killer had ripped them open, scattered seed all over the floor, and then trashed the room before leaving.

[*'PIGEON' GOLDIE IS SLAIN IN HER L.A. HOTEL ROOM,* San Bernadino County Sun, 6 June, 1964]

During the autopsy, the coroner would determine that Goldie had been sexually molested. The L.A.P.D. immediately went on the hunt for the murderer/rapist. They didn't have far to look for their first suspect — 29-year-old Jacques Ehlinger had once also had a room at the Cecil, and was picked up by patrol officer J.W. Everson in Pershing Square the following day. Everson spotted blood stains on Ehlinger's clothing and scratch marks on his face. On closer inspection, it also appeared that somebody had bitten his thumb.

[*POLICE NAB SUSPECT IN 'PIGEON LADY' KILLING,*

Los Angeles Evening Citizen News, June 6, 1964]

The homeless, unemployed laborer strongly protested his innocence, and a polygraph test seemed to bear him out. Yes, he knew Goldie Osgood, Ehlinger admitted, and had been present in the area at the time of her death — but he hadn't killed her.

Goldie Osgood wasn't the first woman to be stabbed to death in the vicinity of the Cecil. Three weeks before, on May 16, a 50-year-old woman named Viva Brown had been murdered at a different hotel, the Rosslyn, a short distance away. She had come to Los Angeles from Oakland in order to attend the horse races. An unknown assailant stabbed her repeatedly, raped her, and strangled her with one of her own stockings.

[*PIGEON WOMAN' IS SLAIN,* Los Angeles Evening Citizen News, 5 June, 1964]

The month prior to that, on April 29, a third woman was viciously killed. Just like Goldie, this victim had also enjoyed feeding the pigeons in MacArthur Park, two miles away. The parallels between the three murders were obvious.

[*SUSPECT HELD IN SLAYING OF BIRD-LOVER,* Independent, Long Beach, June 6, 1964].

Two days after his arrest, the police released Jacques

Ehlinger from custody. Following his interrogation, they came to believe that he was not responsible for the murder of Goldie Osgood. With the trail now growing cold, they had no solid leads to follow up on. Equally frustrating was the fact that Goldie had been seen alive just a few moments before her body was found, indicating that her killer had only narrowly avoided being spotted.

Pershing Park was filled with floral tributes in Goldie's memory, a testament to how beloved she was among the local community. This was a poor area, but despite that fact, the residents pooled their money in order to show their love for one of their own.

Sadly, despite the best efforts of the L.A.P.D., the killer of 'Pigeon' Goldie Osgood was never caught and brought to justice. If he was also responsible for the other rape/murders in the vicinity of the Cecil, which seems likely, then one is forced to wonder just what happened to him. Did this nameless man stop killing because he was jailed for some other crime, moved out of the area, or died himself? The chances are that we will never know.

CHAPTER SIX
Night Stalker

It is safe to say that the 1980s marked a low point for the Hotel Cecil. Drug use, prostitution, and violent crime were all happening both inside and outside its walls. Many of the residents were poor and transient, alternating their days and nights living rough on the streets with stays at the Cecil whenever a little money came their way.

Arguably the hotel's most infamous resident took up occupancy there in 1985: one Richard Ramirez, aka the Night Stalker. Much has been written about Ramirez already. I covered him in my book *Serial Killers: The Minds, Methods, and Mayhem of History's Most Notorious Murderers* (Visible Ink Press, 2021). For a truly comprehensive biography, the reader is referred to Philip Carlo's book *The Night Stalker: The Life and Crimes Of Richard Ramirez.*

Ramirez was born on February 29, 1960, in El Paso, Texas. His mother and father had immigrated to the United States from Mexico. Ramirez's boyhood idol was his older cousin Miguel, who went by the name Mike. Mike was deployed to Vietnam as a member of the U.S. Special

Forces. It was from him that the young and impressionable boy heard lurid stories of firefights in the jungle, and afterwards, of raping and torturing Vietnamese women. These stories were supposedly illustrated by the contents of a box full of graphic photos — photos of the women fellating Mike while he aimed a loaded gun at their heads.

The young Ramirez was almost certainly influenced by the photo of Mike clutching a girl's decapitated head, grinning for the camera. Richard wanted to be like Mike, and when the older man began teaching him how to creep stealthily through the shadows, the boy ate it up. The two bonded closely, but things took an unexpected turn in 1973. Mike's temper got the better of him during a fight with his wife. In a fit of rage, he pulled out a gun and shot her dead. The young Richard Ramirez watched it happen. Afterward, he solemnly promised he would never rat his older cousin out. He never did.

His education as a criminal continued with a move to L.A., where he lived with his brother, Ruben. The older Ramirez was addicted to drugs, and he financed his habit with a life of minor crime. Burglary and theft were his forte, and he taught his younger brother how to case vulnerable houses and break into them without getting caught.

The husband of Richard's sister, Ruth, was a Peeping Tom. He delighted in taking the youthful Ramirez out at night, where the two of them would lurk in the shadows, hoping to catch a glimpse of a woman getting undressed. With each nocturnal expedition, Richard's perverse desires were being fed and growing at the same rate as his criminal tendencies.

Philosophically, Ramirez felt drawn to the teachings of Satanism. The idea of limitless power seemed intoxicating to him, and he soon began to perceive himself as Satan's chosen servant. That offered him a false sense of invincibility, and the belief that Satan would always keep him safe from harm, no matter how much trouble he managed to get himself into. This belief would soon be put to the test when the 22-year-old Ramirez headed west, looking for opportunities in California.

It is believed that Richard Ramirez committed his first murder on April 10, 1984. His victim was a 9-year-old girl named Mei Leung, who lived in an apartment on O'Farrell Street in San Francisco's Tenderloin District. The innocent little girl was playing games with her brother, and suddenly realized that she had dropped some money somewhere along the way. She went looking for it, promising that she would come back. She never did.

The badly beaten little girl's body was found hanging from a water pipe down in the basement. She had been raped, frenziedly stabbed, and then strangled. Always the sadist, Ramirez had left Mei's body hanging just a short distance above the floor. If she had been just a fraction taller, she might have lived — although even if the hanging hadn't killed her, the stabbing probably would have.

For his future rapes and murders, Richard Ramirez would turn his attention to adult victims. The citizens of Los Angeles would soon begin fearing nightfall. On the night of June 28, 1984, he killed a 79-year-old woman named Jennie Vincow. After casing her home from outside, Ramirez made entry via an open window and found her fast asleep in the master bedroom. Pulling out a knife, he repeatedly stabbed the defenseless woman and then cut her throat when she started to scream.

Most fledgling killers would have fled the scene at that point, exhilarated at having killed a victim but afraid that her screams might bring the police. Not so Richard Ramirez, who was convinced that Satan would protect him. He went to the bathroom and cleaned himself up, then turned his experienced burglar's eye on the valuables within the residence. After all, not only did he have to eat, but Richard Ramirez was developing a cocaine habit he had to support.

Nine months passed before he struck again, in the spring of 1985. Ramirez ambushed a 22-year-old woman named Maria Hernandez outside her house, opening fire on her inside the garage with the .22 pistol he'd begun to favor using over a knife. Ramirez, dressed entirely in black, had been cruising around, looking for a victim, and on a whim, he chose Hernandez.

As she got out of her car inside the garage, a dark figure walked up to her, gun extended, and shot her in the face. The victim got a hand up to protect herself, still clutching the car keys, and almost unbelievably, they deflected the small caliber bullet, saving Maria's life in the process.

Leaving her for dead, Ramirez went inside the house and fatally shot her unsuspecting roommate, 34-year-old Dayle Okazki, in the head, then fled. When police officers responded to the scene, Maria was able to describe the man who had killed her roommate and tried to murder her.

Rather than keeping a low profile after killing two victims (or so he thought) Richard Ramirez instead chose to hunt again. Roughly five miles away from the first crime scene, he dragged 30-year-old Tsai-Lian Yu from her car and shot her repeatedly at point blank range.

His next victims were 64-year-old Vincent Zazzara and his wife Maxine. Shooting Vincent first in order to remove the greatest potential threat, he beat, stabbed, and then shot Maxine. The savage attack continued even after she was dead, and in a truly vile finale, Ramirez cut out her eyes as a keepsake.

It has been noted that when Richard Ramirez went home after each killing, he fourteenth floor of the Cecil. The hotel was renowned for having a fairly shady clientele at that particular time in its history, and it's said that nobody batted an eyelid at the lanky, Saturnine man in black when he climbed the staircase up to the top floor. Some stories maintain that, fresh from his latest murder, Ramirez made a habit of peeling off his bloodstained clothes in the alleyway behind the hotel, dropping them where they would draw no more attention than any of Skid Row's other detritus. It was on some of these occasions that he is said to have had to climb the stairs barefoot, clad only in his underwear. Whether there is any actual validity to these accounts is unclear.

The fourteenth floor would have been an ideal place for Ramirez to have gotten a room. Generally, the hotel staff tended to dislike the upper floors, finding the rooms and their occupants to be more dangerous and unstable the higher up they got.

While he was staying at the Cecil for around six weeks prior to his capture, Richard Ramirez used to eat lunch at a Mexican restaurant next door, by the name of Margarita's Place. When interviewed by a reporter from the United Press, the restaurant's cook recalled: "When I looked him in the eyes, he seemed worried about something." We can only surmise what that something might have been. Perhaps the possibility of him being recognized (based upon his description) and turned in to the police?

[*HIGHWAY TO HELL*, Sunday Herald Times, Aurelio Rojas & K. Mack Sisk, September 8, 1985.]

Ramirez is also believed to have rented a room at the Huntington Hotel nearby, but the Cecil seemed to suit him better. Raoul Enriquez, a bartender and waiter at the Cecil, recalled that the Night Stalker liked to blast heavy metal music from his room while getting high on marijuana.

[*'STALKER' SUSPECT CHARGED WITH MURDER, OTHER CRIMES*, Richard de Atley, Associated Press, 4 September 1985]

On May 14, 1985, Ramirez killed a couple named Bill and

Lillian Doi. He broke into their home, and shot 66-year-old Bill, before going after his 56-year-old wife. Lillian had a physical disability, and she couldn't fight her attacker off. Ramirez handcuffed her and took his time sexually assaulting the poor woman while she was completely defenseless. When the brutal attack was over, he took what valuable items he could grab, and disappeared into the night. Mrs. Doi survived the horrific events of that night. Unfortunately, her husband did not.

All through the summer of 1985, many Californians lived in a state of near-permanent fear once the sun went down. Emboldened by the fact that the police hadn't come anywhere close to catching him yet, and still utterly convinced that Satan was acting as his Get Out of Jail Free Card, Richard Ramirez continued his string of sex attacks and violent assaults.

He raped two senior citizens, 83-year-old Mabel Bell and 81-year-old Florence Lang, after breaking into their home late one night. Neither was capable of putting up a fight. Ramirez didn't care. Tying them both up, he took sadistic pleasure in torturing them both, taking the time to draw a pentagram on the thigh of one.

Carol Kyle, a 42-year-old nurse, was attacked in her

Burbank home while her 11-year-old son was tied up in the closet. This was one of Ramirez's most depraved and sickening sexual assaults yet, and Carol Kyle endured it without complaint in the hope that her assailant would spare the lives of herself and her son. Incredibly, he did.

Now, thanks to the media, he had a nickname: *The Valley Intruder.* This pandered to his ego, and only served to bolster Ramirez's belief in his own invulnerability. Unbeknownst to him, however, that arrogance would soon lead to his downfall.

On July 2, Ramirez murdered 75-year-old widow Mary Louise Cannon, slitting her throat and stabbing her. In a break from his usual modus operandi, he did not sexually assault Mrs. Cannon, but he did burglarize her home. The violence inflicted upon his next victim, a 61-year-old woman named Joyce Lucille Nelson, also did not fit the usual Ramirez M.O. He chose to forego weapons entirely and instead battered her to death.

As the home invasions mounted and a sense of general unease grew, the so-called Valley Intruder was given a new name. People began to call him the Night Stalker, after he told one terrified victim that this was his name. The police presence throughout the L.A. area was stepped up significantly after dark, but Richard Ramirez was not deterred. He continued to leave the Hotel Cecil at night to search for vulnerable homes to break into, returning to his room on the fourteenth floor after each attack.

Ultimately, every serial killer's luck runs out, and so it was with Richard Ramirez. He was seen by a 13-year-old boy, as he was driving slowly through his neighborhood on the way to commit his next crime. Ramirez had a mocking, evil-looking face, framed with lank, stringy hair. His sallow appearance was ghoulish enough that the boy remembered it clearly, and he was able to describe the car the man was driving to police officers, along with a fragment of its plate number. This was exactly the break the police needed. They were able to track the car down and fingerprint it.

The print of one Richard Ramirez was lifted cleanly off the rear-view mirror. Based on the length of his rap sheet, the cops knew that 25-year-old Ramirez was a petty criminal at the very least, and he seemed like a good fit for the Night Stalker. The only question was: where did he live?

Los Angeles and its surrounding areas are a jostling warren of humanity. On the one hand, looking for Richard Ramirez would be like hunting for a needle in a haystack, detectives thought. On the other, it increased the likelihood that if the public was made aware of his appearance, sooner or later *somebody* was going to run into him.

Newspapers and TV stations were sent copies of Ramirez's photograph, along with the news that he was a person of interest in the Night Stalker attacks. In fact, Ramirez wasn't just a person of interest; he was *the* person of interest.

On Saturday, August 31, in a store in East L.A., Richard Ramirez found himself looking at his own face, the familiar cold, dead eyes staring back at him from the newspaper stand. He knew, right then and there, that the game was up. Ramirez turned to leave. He didn't make it far before he was recognized. A crowd began to follow him, growing by the minute.

It was payback time. People who had lived in fear of Richard Ramirez now took it in turns to batter him, punching and kicking, knocking him to the ground. Some even used improvised weapons. In an irony of ironies, officers of the L.A.P.D. saved the blood-splattered Night Stalker from the grip of the people he had tortured and abused for so long. Ramirez had come closer than he realized to getting lynched, shot, or simply beaten to death on the streets of L.A. Many would have said that he had gotten his just desserts.

He would never set foot inside the Hotel Cecil ever again.

After a long and dramatic trial, Richard Ramirez was sentenced to death. Apparently, Satan was either sleeping on the job, or had suddenly lost his desire to protect the Night Stalker.

Fulfillment of that sentence was not quick in coming. Richard Ramirez languished on death row until 2013, when at the age of 53, cancer killed him before the executioner was given a chance.

His connection with the Hotel Cecil is now well known, and it has been good fodder for tour guides in Los Angeles for many years. To answer one fairly obvious question: there is no evidence at all to suggest that any of his victims came back to the hotel with him and were killed there. Ramirez preferred to do his killing in the home of his victim, or on one rare occasion, the street outside.

Yet his room has a reputation for having a malevolent atmosphere — hardly surprising, when we consider the nature of its occupant for a stretch in the mid-1980s. Does Richard Ramirez haunt the Hotel Cecil? Despite what you may have seen on *American Horror Story: Hotel*, no, he does not. At least, I have yet to see any compelling evidence to indicate that this might be the case.

CHAPTER SEVEN
Unterweger

Much has been made of the link between Richard Ramirez and the Hotel Cecil. Less commonly known is the fact that another serial killer also stayed there. Austrian Johann Unterweger — who also went by Jack — was a reporter who came to the United States in 1991, and stayed at the Cecil while he ostensibly worked on a story about the seamer side of life in L.A., especially prostitution.

In reality, Jack Unterweger was far more deeply involved in the dark side of Los Angeles than journalism. He took a sadistic pleasure in murdering three of the sex workers who crossed his path.

As a younger man, the 24-year-old Unterweger strangled 18-year-old Margaret Schafer to death, after first battering her with a metal bar. In what would become a signature habit, Unterweger used his victim's own bra as a murder weapon. Caught and tried for her killing, he was sentenced to life in prison.

It wasn't his first stretch inside. He already had a criminal history for offenses as varied as theft, rape, and prostitution. This would, however, be his longest sentence at fifteen years. On the inside, Unterweger worked hard to better himself...or so it appeared. He read voraciously, and used his ample free time to write poetry, plays, and fiction. Unlike other prisoners, he obeyed the rules and he didn't cause problems. He simply kept quiet and did his time.

It was believed at the time that as an author, Johann Unterweger was no hack. Even some of the most ardent literary critics agreed that his work was of a very high standard. He poured a lot of his anger and resentment into his writing. If his story was to be believed, then his childhood had been a miserable one. Young Johann was abandoned at an early age by his father, an American soldier, and suffered physical abuse while he was growing up. He also spent time in a series of orphanages. The boy's suffering was described in an autobiography he wrote while incarcerated. Years later, it would emerge that a number of details in the book were fabricated, probably in a shrewd attempt to manipulate the public's perception of him, and also to generate sympathy and support for his release.

Unterweger was eventually released in 1990. Surprisingly, he became something of a media personality. His writings were popular, and it wasn't long before the charismatic murderer was given the opportunity to be a guest star on several TV shows. Soon, he would even be allowed to front them himself.

Plenty of cash. Expensive clothes. A flashy car. Adoration from the public and even the literati. The murderer turned writer had it all.

Johann Unterweger had succeeded in fooling everybody into thinking that he had turned over a new leaf. There had even been a petition with the intention of getting him released early, and a lot of influential people had thrown their support behind it.

Had he truly been rehabilitated, had he really gone straight, then this was Johann Unterweger's chance to put his murky past behind him and start afresh, making a genuine success of his life.

Of course, that's not what happened. In reality, he had gone straight back to killing prostitutes. His preferred method of murder, strangulation with the victim's own bra, made it clear to investigators that the killings were linked, but in 1990, nobody connected them with the release of Johann Unterweger from prison. The bodies of the dead women were dumped in forests and on hillsides.

Why his fascination with and hatred for prostitutes? It has been speculated that it originated with Unterweger's mother, who was one herself, as was his aunt, murdered by an enraged male customer— or so he claimed. There's doubt as to whether she actually existed. He would later claim to have seen his mother's face superimposed over that of his first victim as he strangled her to death. As a boy, Unterweger spent his life around prostitutes, and most likely developed his attitude toward them during these formative years.

In the summer of 1991, the offer of a trip to the United States in order to write about American crime for Austrian magazines was a dream come true. It offered him a fresh hunting ground, new opportunities to lure and kill prostitutes. Unterweger accepted it without hesitation, and after flying in to L.A., he took up residence at the Hotel Cecil between June 11 and July 16 — although there was a brief period where he moved out of the hotel and stayed in Hollywood.

The L.A.P.D. was only too happy to help this charming journalist from overseas, and they set him up with a ride-along in one of their patrol units. Jack Unterweger got a first-hand look at the interactions between the police officers and the sex workers.

Throughout June and July, he murdered three sex workers, strangling each one and dumping their bodies in isolated locations. The police knew that one of the dead women, a 33- year-old named Irene Rodriguez, often solicited johns in the area surrounding the Cecil and other nearby hotels.

Detectives did not connect any of the murders with the journalist staying at the Cecil, the nice man who had seemed so interested in their experiences and their procedures. Jack Unterweger returned to Austria shortly afterward. Unbeknownst to him, in his absence, the eight murders he had committed before coming to America were now starting to point toward him as the possible killer.

With law enforcement closing in, Unterweger got squirrelly and fled, taking his 18-year-old girlfriend, Bianca Mrak, along with him. He led European police on a merry chase, flitting from one country to the next, finally ending up back where he'd started: the United States. Every so often, he would contact the media and insist that he was an innocent man, one who was being unfairly maligned because of a crime for which he had already paid his debt to society.

His luck finally ran out in Florida. Detectives were able to locate him by means of his credit card receipts. He was duly arrested and then extradited back to Austria in order to answer for his crimes, against the wishes of the L.A.P.D., who wanted him tried Stateside. Had he so wished,

Unterweger had the right to oppose his extradition, but perhaps understandably, he chose not to. After all, Austria had no death penalty on the books, whereas conviction in the state of California would likely have sent him to the gas chamber or given him the lethal injection.

As things turned out, it was a moot point. In June 1994, a jury in Graz found Jack Unterweger guilty of nine murders, including the three women he had killed in L.A., and once again sentenced him to life imprisonment. The trial was interrupted when a bomb exploded outside the courthouse, causing serious damage. The identity of the bomber remains unknown.

At 3:40am the following morning, prison officers found him hanging from a curtain rod in his cell. The serial killer had used a cord from his pants as a means to escape spending the rest of his life behind bars.

Over the course of four years, newpaper headlines had gone from calling Unterweger "the Prison Poet" to referring to him as "the Austrian Ripper." Some have speculated that he was overcome by dark forces at the Cecil Hotel and was influenced by them to go out and kill. It's easy to dismiss this ridiculous theory out of hand. Johann Unterweger liked killing. He got off on taking the lives of women. That was established long before he ever got off the plane at L.A.X. and headed for the hotel on South Main. Although his presence at the Cecil is now firmly rooted in its dark lore, nothing about the place motivated him to murder, because that was his planned intent all along.

Then there are the people who claim that Unterwenger killed his three female victims in his hotel room. It is highly unlikely that he murdered any of his victims at the Cecil, or even brought them back there. For one thing, after the three women had been fatally strangled, how would their killer have gotten their dead body out of the building without being seen? While Skid Row and the Cecil were lawless places back in 1991, they weren't *that* lawless.

Also, why would Unterweger have run the risk of bringing the women back to his room, knowing full well that they would soon turn up dead? All it would have taken was one resident to recognize the murdered woman's picture, recall seeing her in the company of the Austrian man at the Cecil, and then report it to the police. The game would have been up.

No, far safer to keep them well away from his place of residence and cut down on the number of potential witnesses. The likelihood is that Jack Unterweger picked his victims up in his car, drove them to isolated locations on the pretext of paying them for sex, then beat and killed them there, before dumping the bodies and leaving the scene. Some of the bodies lay undisturbed long enough to badly decompose in the summer heat.

I have heard no accounts of anything paranormal associated with Johann Unterweger's stay at the Cecil, and I strongly suspect that this vile and odious individual is nothing more than a dark stain on the pages of the hotel's history books.

[*AUSTRIAN AUTHOR UNTERWEGER FOUND DEAD IN HIS PRISON CELL*, St. Cloud Times, 29 June, 1994]

[*AUSTRIAN STILL SUSPECT IN 3 KILLINGS,* Los Angeles Times, 3 April 1992 (Eric Malnic)]

[*SLAYER OF L.A. PROSTITUTES KILLS HIMSELF IN AUSTRIAN PRISON CELL,* Los Angeles Times, 30 June 1994 (Eric Malnic)]

[https://www.independent.co.uk/news/world/murderer-s-final-freedom-the-bizarre-life-of-jack-unterweger-poet-and-killer-of-prostitutes-ends-at-his-own-hand-1417861.html]

CHAPTER EIGHT
Elisa

And so, here we are. We've finally arrived at the part of the book which covers the incident for which the Cecil is most famous (or should I say infamous): the death of Elisa Lam.

So much has been written about this young woman's mysterious and tragic fate, it's hard to find a great deal that's new to say about it. Enter Elisa's name, or that of the Hotel Cecil, into any search engine, and the unwary browser may soon find themselves going down rabbit hole after rabbit hole, following the tangled threads that link one conspiracy theory to another.

The world is, of course, full of armchair experts, thanks largely to the Internet, and just who am I to get on my high horse? I may be a writer, but I'm also no more qualified than anybody else to render a verdict on what really happened to her on her last day alive. I'm not a homicide detective or a forensic pathologist. So, at the risk of giving offense, let me put it bluntly: I do not know exactly how Elisa Lam died...and the likelihood is that neither do you.

I have an opinion, and we all know what they say about those. Before arriving at that opinion, I studied the circumstances surrounding Elisa Lam's life and death, trying to piece together what I think might have happened. But at the end of the day, this chapter of the book will not tell you with any certainty how this unfortunate young woman met her fate, because *nobody knows*. Even the experts, the homicide detectives and coroners, have their doubts. I therefore ask you, before we go any further, to set your preconceptions aside, lower your expectations, and expect great uncertainty from this part of the book. It is impossible to tie this case up into a neat little bow, much as we would like to. The chances are that it will never be solved to everybody's satisfaction, and at the end of the day, all that we have is the evidence…and conjecture.

Elisa Lam had always wanted to travel, and at the age of twenty-one, the world was her oyster. A tour of the American West Coast beckoned. Like so many hopefuls before her, the young woman from Vancouver arrived in Los Angeles with a little disposable income, lots of dreams, and a desire to see the *real* L.A.

One thing she did *not* have were ambitions to become an

actress, sell a movie or TV script, or otherwise make it big in the entertainment industry, which set her apart from a lot of visitors, many of whom came to L.A. with fantasies of Hollywood stardom. She was just a tourist, with no real pretensions, other than a wish to discover California and perhaps something of herself at the same time.

After crossing San Diego off her itinerary, Los Angeles was her next stop. In the Cecil she found an affordable and convenient place to stay, in a centralized location. Sure, the neighborhood may not have been the greatest, but on the plus side, there was a bookstore nearby, somewhere, which would cater to her love of reading. She took a room there on January 28.

The Cecil had undergone something of an identity change in 2011, switching its name to the Stay on Main...or, more accurately, the building was divided structurally, but not much else changed. This was most likely an attempt to separate the building from its checkered past, by posing it as a new and different entity. Yet little was different. The building was the same. Despite the cosmetic name change, the signs outside still read "CECIL HOTEL." Those signs, each of which is 70 feet tall, can still be found on the northwest and southwest corners. Both are original to the building, and they have been there since it was built in 1924. The long-term residents of the hotel were clustered on their own floors, but they shared common elevators with the more temporary guests.

Browsing the Internet, looking for deals, it was likely that the casual traveler who happened upon the Stay on Main website would have thought they had struck gold. The room rates were cheap, especially for a hotel in downtown Los Angeles — almost suspiciously cheap, in fact. As with so many things in life, if it looks too good to be true, then it usually is.

The Stay at Main was one hundred percent the Hotel Cecil, despite the fact that its lobby and reception desk had gotten spruced up a little and given a facelift. Browse its website, and the Stay on Main doesn't look too bad at all.

(https://www.agoda.com/en-za/stay-on-main-hotel/hotel/los-angeles-ca-us.html?cid=1841944&tag=14073816_8378930_).

The lobby and common areas look quite elegant, while the guest rooms appear, to coin a phrase, "cheap and cheerful." Unless you did a little research, you would have no idea that by booking a room there, you would be staying at L.A.'s infamous "murder hotel," as some liked to call it.

Three days later, she disappeared. Her parents were worried. Elisa checked in with them regularly, usually calling at least once a day to let them know she was alright. It wasn't like her to go off the grid like that without a word of warning.

She was declared missing on February 1. Elisa had stated her intention to check out that day. Things hadn't gone well for her during her brief stay at the Cecil. Initially, she stayed in a room on the fifth floor, #506, which she shared with several other female guests. While there, Elisa behaved in ways that her roommates found sufficiently strange that they asked for her to be moved. Hotel management dutifully moved her to a single room.

It wasn't just her roommates that had witnessed Elisa acting strangely. She had gone to the recording of a TV show, during which she is said to have been so disruptive that security guards removed her from the studio, and later caused a scene in the hotel lobby with an irrational outburst.

Red flags went up when it was found that Elisa's belongings were still present in her room. The room itself was a mess, but it didn't appear to have been ransacked — this was disorder, not destruction, something that hotel cleaning staff see all the time. Although her phone was gone, almost everything else, including her cash, cards, computer, and the passport she would ultimately need to get home, had all been abandoned.

Elisa Lam hadn't checked out. She had vanished.

People disappear every day. Thousands drop off the grid each year. Some return, some don't. Some simply don't want to be found. In the case of Elisa Lam, the possibilities of her having gotten lost in L.A., or deliberately taking off without telling anybody, were soon discounted. Something just didn't seem right about the manner of her disappearance, and the police took it seriously from the outset.

The missing persons investigation brought a slew of detectives to the Cecil. Staff and guests alike were asked questions. Detectives wanted to know when Elisa was last seen alive, and they were especially interested in whether anybody was with her. It soon became clear that the final sighting of her had come from a hotel employee, who moved her away from a restricted section and watched Elisa head in the direction of the elevators. She was alone at the time.

The hotel's CCTV camera system offered a baffling new clue as to her last known movements. She was picked up by a camera mounted inside one of the elevators. Elisa was acting bizarrely, moving in an unusual way that suggested she might be either talking to somebody or avoiding them. If somebody else *was* present, that individual never entered the camera's field of vision. Either they were a flesh and blood person who chose not to step close to the elevator, or Elisa Lam was talking to somebody that nobody else could see.

She was seen to push multiple buttons, one after the other, her body language suggesting that she was anxious. The doors didn't close for quite some time, which is actually normal for that particular elevator car. Sticking her head out into the hallway, Elisa looked to either side, then pressed herself into the corner next to the elevator car's control panel, before once again scanning the hallway outside. Just who, or what, was she looking for?

Elisa stepped back out of the elevator. Her movements were jerky, almost puppet-like. She once again bent over and started mashing button after button. This was not, by any stretch of the imagination, everyday, rational behavior. She began to gesticulate, as though pleading with somebody outside the elevator that was out of frame. The hand motions got wilder, until Elisa began to look like the conductor of an orchestra, or a conjuror casting a spell, and then she abruptly walked away.

Unfortunately, once Elisa Lam had disappeared from the

camera's view, she was never seen alive again.

The police still had no real leads to follow. They appealed to the public for help, and got nowhere. The CCTV footage made them confident of just one thing: Elisa Lam had not left the hotel through any of the exits, which were covered by its cameras...ergo, she had to still be somewhere inside its walls.

A handful of officers searched the hotel, going floor by floor, checking one room after the next. They opened closets, peered under beds, and looked everywhere in which a body might conceivably be found. They went up to the roof, and while they did look around up there, none of the officers gave a thought to the four huge tanks that supplied the hotel with its water.

That would prove to be their biggest mistake.

With the search effectively going nowhere, the L.A.P.D. released the footage of Elisa inside the elevator to the public. It went viral, becoming an overnight sensation. People found it by turns chilling, compelling, perplexing, and fascinating. Something about the four minutes of film is reminiscent of a horror movie. Indeed, parallels would later be made with the 2005 film *Dark Water,* starring Jennifer Connelly, to name just one.

An army of armchair sleuths mobilized seemingly overnight, banding together in online forums across the Internet and going over every single frame of the video in minute, painstaking detail. Was Elisa Lam on the run from an assailant, they asked? Was she being tormented by the restless spirits of those who had died at the Hotel Cecil? Or could her behavior be explained away by something as simple as a behavioral emergency, alcohol intoxication, or some kind of drug use? What about an occult-themed game of some sort?

On 19 February, almost three weeks after she was reported missing, guests at the Cecil called the front desk to complain about the water. The pressure was low, they said. It was a strange, dark color. Most concerning of all, it had an odd taste.

A hotel employee was sent to the roof to check the four 1,000-gallon water storage tanks. Climbing up on top of the tanks, he looked down into the open hatch of one. Inside was the partially decomposed body of Elisa Lam, floating face up in the water.

Thanks to the Internet, there are now thousands of self-appointed experts on the life and death of Elisa Lam. To an extent, many of them see what they want to see. Some have an interest in the paranormal, and they bring that particular bias to their theories on what happened. There are sensational stories of the Cecil's ghosts haunting her, taunting her, playing games with her mind.

Some have said that Elisa was possessed by an evil spirit; others claim that she was playing the so-called "Elevator Game," pushing buttons in a very specific sequence in order to gain access to the spirit world.

Is the Hotel Cecil haunted? I certainly think so. Does that haunting have anything at all to do with the death of Elisa Lam? There's not a shred of evidence to support the idea, and frankly, it does a disservice to her memory to propagate those stories in the absence of proof.

Many people have asked why the elevator doors remained open for as long as they did. A number of possible reasons have been floated for this, with some people claiming that an unseen attacker was somehow preventing the elevator from moving. Rob Hernandez, a paranormal investigator who visited the Hotel Cecil himself in order to research claims of it being haunted, confirmed that the elevator has a hold button. He believes that it is one of the buttons that Elisa pushed when she entered the car, and he adds that pressing it will keep the elevator in place for a minimum of two minutes.

Another frequently asked question is: how did Elisa's body get up to the roof? I suspect that she climbed the fire escape. As part of the initial search of the hotel, police K9 units joined in, deploying sniffer dogs to hunt down Elisa's scent. They found it outside her room, and followed the scent along a hallway, where it dead-ended at a window. The window opened out onto the fire escape, which led down to the street, or up to the roof.

Even more ubiquitous than the ghost stories are the murder theories. Some claim that a member of the hotel staff killed Elisa, then put her body in the rooftop water tank. Variants on this story have somebody else committing the murder, but having an employee acting as an accomplice, along with a complicit Los Angeles Police Department. The further one goes down this particular road, the wilder the stories get. I won't take up further space recounting them here. They could fill entire books by themselves. They have already taken up countless hours of YouTube video footage.

It has to be said that there *are* some unusual elements

surrounding her death. Some have pointed out that the coroner's autopsy finding changed state from *could not be determined* to *accident*. This shouldn't necessarily be seen as a red flag. Coroners are fallible, too. They make mistakes. Unfortunately, this particular error has fueled several conspiracy theories, all of them having foul play as their theme.

I don't pretend to know the truth behind Elisa Lam's death. Having studied the circumstances surrounding it, I do have an opinion, but I'm perfectly willing to admit that I'm susceptible to biases of my own, just as everybody is. One might expect somebody like me, a paranormal investigator and author, to come down on the side of the ghost-related theories. In fact, nothing could be further from the truth.

I have spent the past nineteen years of my life working in the field of Emergency Medicine. In that time, I have seen and treated many patients who are experiencing behavioral crises. As previously mentioned, Elisa Lam had a documented history of depression and bipolar disorder. As a diagnosed depressive myself, one who requires medication in order to function, I have a great deal of sympathy for her. What was supposed to have been her life's greatest adventure, ultimately led to Elisa spending her last days in a place like the Cecil. Emergency sirens going past at all hours of the day and night. A constant flow of strangers, some friendly, some not so friendly. Drug abuse, violence, and squalor all around. The very definition of hyper-stimulation.

It would have been daunting, at best, and it's easy to see how the pressure might have gotten to her. Some commentators have proposed that Elisa's odd behavior on the elevator video might be put down to somebody having drugged her, perhaps with a date rape drug such as Rohypnol. The toxicology screen detected no evidence of such a drug in her bloodstream. The levels of her antidepressants and bipolar disorder treatment medications, on the other hand, were *low*. In other words, it is likely that she was either off her medications, or at least not taking them consistently. That, in turn, makes it increasingly likely that she suffered a psychotic episode on the night of her death, causing her to act in an irrational and unpredictable way.

One potential side effect of bipolar psychosis is hallucination, seeing and hearing things that aren't actually there. Another is paranoia. In the elevator video, Elisa appears to be worried about something outside in the hallway. At times, she acts as if she's being pursued.

In such a state, could Elisa Lam have climbed the fire escape up to the roof of the Cecil and climbed into the water tank? Could her altered mental status have rendered her incapable of escape?

Absolutely.

We don't need ghosts, murderers, or elaborate conspiracies to explain her death. A behavioral disorder, exacerbated by a lack of medication and a stressful, unfamiliar environment, are in my view, constitute the simplest and most logical explanation. This is further supported by the bizarre behavior that caused her roommates to complain, and the emotional outburst Elisa underwent in the lobby of the hotel.

It is my belief that Ockham's Razor, the time-honored principle that the simplest explanation usually tends to be the right one, applies in this case.

The loss of a young woman in the prime of her life is an absolute tragedy. Although I cannot prove it, I am convinced that the root cause of this was Elisa Lam's underlying medical condition. We should not tarnish this by making it out to be some kind of dark and twisted fairytale, a macabre horror story straight out of a Stephen King novel.

We owe her memory better than that.

CHAPTER NINE
Ghosts

After so many decades of history and heartache, the Cecil Hotel, aka the Stay on Main, was closed down for the short term on January 1, 2017.

Simon Baron Development is a real estate property development firm based out of New York City. In 2016, the company had acquired rights to the property at 640 S. Main Street, Los Angeles, with a view to transforming the Cecil into something far removed from its tarnished past. On their website, the company states:

The property, currently positioned as a budget hotel, will undergo an extensive capital improvement program and be repositioned into a state of the art mixed use facility.

What does that mean, in real world terms? Firstly, a part of the structure will be converted into a boutique hotel, which is industry parlance for a relatively small (ten to one hundred room) hotel that is fitted out in a very specific style, and contains what realtors like to describe as Unique Selling Points, or USPs. Such hotels are rather exclusive, usually with room prices to match, and are frequented by those who seek a non-traditional type of hotel experience – and are willing to pay for it.

That still leaves a lot of space to fill. The plans are for the addition of some three hundred micro-apartments. As the name implies, these are small, single-room residences, often owned or let by young professionals. Micro-apartments usually don't run larger than 200-300 square feet, especially in high-demand areas. The question remains, however: how popular are they going to be, in a neighborhood with the reputation of Skid Row? Unless the area undergoes some form of urban gentrification, how likely is it that people will want to live in a place renowned for drugs, violence, and homelessness?

One of the first things that Simon Baron did after acquiring the Cecil was to petition for it to be listed as a Los Angeles historic-cultural monument. In what proved to be a unanimous vote of ten for and zero against, the application was successful. A strong case was made for the Cecil being a classic example of early twentieth century Los Angeles hotel architecture, something which exemplified that particular place and time in history. On that basis, its place on the map of L.A. has been assured for the foreseeable future.

At the time of writing, it is not possible to get a room at the Stay on Main. Even before the Covid-19 pandemic hit, the hotel had shut its doors to paying guests in order to undergo remodeling and refurbishment.

I wanted to get a sense of what it was like to stay inside the hotel, and that knowledge ultimately came from two sources. One was an interview with ghost hunter Rob Hernandez, who spent time at the Cecil looking for...well, ghosts. The other was a very illuminating blog post by a gentleman named Joey DeVilla, who stayed there while attending an I.T. conference back in 2008. I highly encourage you to read Joey's account in full. Titled *A Dump with a Future,* you can find it over at his website, Joey DeVilla.com.

Spoilers: it does *not* paint a very flattering picture.

Joey ended up at the Cecil totally by accident. Staying there was to be an experience he would never forget.

It's important to remember that he visited several years before the death of Elisa Lam placed the hotel squarely back in the public eye. It didn't have the national reputation back then that it would soon go on to acquire.

A sign announcing that no visitors were allowed to accompany guests upstairs didn't unduly alarm him. He figured that the rule was in place to stop prostitutes venturing up to the guest rooms. Having seen the neighborhood surrounding the hotel, that didn't seem like an unreasonable concern.

On his way up to his room, Joey noticed that there were communal toilets and showers. The hotel had plainly seen better days. His room was serviceable (just about) but also was definitely on the cheaper, more cramped side of acceptability, even for the relatively low price he'd paid. When he was waiting to check out, Joey found himself witnessing a verbal altercation between hotel staff and a one-legged man in a wheelchair — presumably one of the many semi-permanent residents to whom the Cecil was a home away from home.

After conceding that the lobby is gorgeous, he concluded that most of the hotel was "craptacular." Mr. DeVilla may have been surprised when a poster claiming to be part of the hotel's management company took him to task for his largely negative review. However, his blog post does an excellent job in capturing the feel of staying at the Cecil toward the end of its natural lifetime, and I highly recommend checking it out, for the accompanying pictures if nothing else.

[https://www.joeydevilla.com/2008/11/03/a-dump-with-a-future-or-my-review-of-the-cecil-hotel-los-angeles/]

Something that Mr. Devilla didn't seem to encounter during his visit were ghosts. Somewhere along the way, the Cecil has developed a reputation for being haunted. It's fair to say that some of the reports are more compelling than others.

Take, for example, the case of musician and TikTok content creator Peet Montzingo, who lives directly across the street from the hotel. It fills the view from his window whenever he happens to look outside, and as such, he keeps a close eye on goings-on inside the building. Unsurprisingly, he reports having seen more than a few weird things during his tenancy.

In an interview with website The Tab [*I LIVE OPPOSITE THE CECIL HOTEL AND THIS IS WHAT IT'S REALLY LIKE THERE,* by Hayley Soen, February 2021] he spills the beans on some of those bizarre occurrences.

According to Montzingo, he has seen unusual lights in some of the Cecil's windows, and has watched doors open and close by themselves in rooms that were empty. Fans and room lights are said to switch themselves off and on. He even claims to have seen human figures walking around in there, and one night, watched an old man sitting in one of the rooms, smoking and watching the world go by. Montzingo found himself getting a serious case of the creeps because his own apartment was in darkness, and so the man should not have been able to see him, and yet as he walked from one window to the next, the smoker turned his head to follow.

He had seen nobody go into or come out of the Cecil for weeks.

Montzingo adds that just walking around the hotel gives him "bad vibes," and that it did so even before he knew of its disturbing history.

One particularly heart-stopping incident occurred when he looked outside and saw a young woman standing in one of the open windows. She looked eerily like Elisa Lam. Concerned that she might be suicidal and about to jump — a very reasonable suspicion, given the hotel's track record — he called out and asked whether she needed help. 911 had been called, and paramedics quickly arrived on scene.

The mystery was quickly solved when the woman turned out to be an actress...shooting for the TV show *Ghost Adventures.*

When the Discovery+ streaming service first debuted in January 2021, one of the tentpole programs was a two-hour special episode of *Ghost Adventures.* If you're unfamiliar with the show, it features a small group of men who visit haunted locations and film one another conducting their own form of paranormal investigation. The long-lived show has been immensely popular, not just on the Travel Channel in the United States, but also in many other countries around the world. Host Zak Bagans and his "Ghost Adventures Crew" have visited more than a hundred allegedly haunted locations during the show's run, and in the process, have also built a loyal and devoted fanbase.

In the world of paranormal "reality" television, *Ghost Adventures* is undeniably one of the heavy hitters — if not *the* heavy hitter, ratings-wise. Bagans is an influential personality in the field, and it's likely that only somebody with his clout and resources would be able to get access to the Cecil in order to shoot there.

I won't spend time dissecting the episode here. The likelihood is that many *Ghost Adventures* loyalists will believe most, if not all, of what is presented to them during the episode, whereas people of a more skeptical nature (or those who simply don't like the show and its approach) will dismiss everything out of hand. The truth most likely can be found somewhere in the middle. I encourage you to watch the episode for yourself, if you are able to do so, and to make up your own mind. No matter what your stance when it comes to *Ghost Adventures,* it's worth your time just to get a look behind the scenes of the Cecil's tightly locked doors. However, please be aware that the show includes graphic recreations of a baby being dropped from an upper window, the blood-splattered bodies of suicide victims laying on the sidewalk, and other potentially disturbing visuals.

(For an interview with Bagans concerning his experiences at the Cecil, see https://www.denofgeek.com/culture/ghost-adventures-cecil-house-zak-bagans-interview/)

During the researching of this book, I waited through a lot of articles and vlogs pertaining to ghostly activity at the Cecil, including one photograph that purported to be an apparition outside one of the hotel's upper windows. The picture was so grainy, it was hard to make out anything of note, let alone a ghost. It is all grist for the mill when it comes to the Cecil's black reputation, but I found very little material that I would classify as solid evidence.

Yet one account stood out from the others. It was decades old, and had been passed on from father to daughter, but was no less compelling for that.

When Joy Johnston was researching her family tree, she discovered something interesting in her father Patrick's naturalization record. He was naturalized as a U.S. citizen on 14 May, 1965. There's nothing particularly significant about that. What stood out to her, though, was the address.

640 South Main Street, Los Angles, California.

Although the legal document doesn't list it by name, this is, of course, the address of the Hotel Cecil. Back then, it wasn't unusual for working men without families to reside in hotels on a semi-permanent basis. That usually changed when they got married and had a family, but while they were still single or family-free, such men often found it cheaper and more convenient to rent a hotel room than a house.

Such was the case with Patrick Johnston.

Joy is the author of *The Reluctant Caregiver*, a book which chronicles her experiences caring for her mom following her diagnosis of colon cancer, following her father's death from Alzheimer's. Joy and I get together for a long-distance interview one afternoon, and I'm quickly impressed with not only her fortitude and resilience, but the positive attitude she somehow managed to keep throughout it all.

Patrick Johnston had quite the terrifying experience one night at the Cecil. Joy recalls clearly that when he told her the story, he would relive the incident all over again, radiating a fear so strong it was almost palpable to his audience.

As he related the incident to his daughter, he woke up suddenly in the dead of night, drenched in sweat. Attempting to sit up, he came to the alarming realization that he was incapable of moving. His body would no longer obey his commands.

Lying there, presumably trying his very best not to panic, Patrick felt what he would later describe as hands closing around his neck, tightening their grip on his throat. Then they began to squeeze. His chest felt heavy, as though something was sitting on top of it. He was barely able to draw in any air, and he felt the awful sensation of being completely unable to breathe.

Finally, after what must have seemed like an eternity, Mr. Johnston regained control of his body. He did what any other rational person would do under those circumstances. He ran.

Understandably frightened, he fled the room and made his way down to the lobby, where he told the clerk working at the front desk what had just happened to him.

If he expected to be laughed at, or dismissed out of hand, Patrick Johnston would have been surprised at the clerk's reaction. He simply shrugged, and then replied that this particular room had recently been the scene of a murder.

Although we don't know which room Mr. Johnston was staying in at the time, it is possible to make an educated guess. We know that 'Pigeon' Goldie Osgood was murdered at the Cecil on Thursday, June 4, 1964 — a little less than a year before Patrick Johnston checked in. She was not only stabbed in the chest, but her killer used a hand towel to choke her to death.

Had Mr. Johnston experienced some kind of residual after-echo from the day of her murder? If his experience was paranormal in nature, as it may well have been, then his sleeping mind might have acted as a receiver, picking up on the psychic residue of that vicious crime. He suffered the feeling of hands locked tightly around his throat, cutting off his air supply and preventing him from breathing. The similarity between that and the way in which Goldie Osgood was killed, is in my opinion a little too close to be written off as mere coincidence.

It should be made clear that Mr. Johnston never sought any publicity or notoriety from sharing his story. He never approached the media, or tried to gain financially from it in any way. To him, this was a frightening and unexplainable experience to tell his family about, his so-called "haunted hotel story."

Skeptics are likely to point out that all of the physical symptoms — the cold sweat, the temporary inability to move a muscle, even the feeling of being choked — may point toward hypnopompic sleep paralysis as a possible explanation. This is a type of natural paralysis that occurs when a person has just woken up, is not yet fully awake, and has still to shrug off the physical effects of being asleep. When we're in deep REM (Rapid Eye Movement) sleep, our muscles are effectively switched off. This is a good thing. Without it, we might hurl ourselves out of bed during a nightmare, or unknowingly inflict serious harm on the person sleeping alongside us.

The most curious thing, however, would be the previous events which took place in that room the year before. We must bear in mind that Mr. Johnston only learned of the room's macabre history *after* the incident, rather than before, and so the backstory could not have subconsciously influenced him. Is it possible that he had heard about Goldie Osgood's murder before checking into the Cecil? Certainly. He read newspapers, after all; but then, what would be the likelihood of him being assigned the very same room in which she was killed?

Patrick Johnston rightly demanded that he be given a new

room, and it would be hard to blame him for that. As far as we know, the rest of his stay at the Cecil passed peacefully and without incident.

This brush with something unseen and violent would stay with Patrick Johnston until his dying day. On the occasions when he recounted the story, he found it physically difficult to complete, because it took him back to that night in a possibly haunted room at 640 South Main Street in Los Angeles.

Was he delusional? Imagining things? I find that explanation possible, but unlikely. Having spoken to Joy, her father was not prone to having an excessively vivid imagination. Yes, he had nightmares, as everybody does from time to time, and some of them were violent in nature, but none of them matched what he had suffered in the Cecil that night. Nor did he ever report experiencing an episode of possible sleep paralysis again.

Joy shared her father's experience via her blog in 2012, the year before Elisa Lam's disappearance and death thrust the hotel into the spotlight again. A number of comments that were received on that particular entry purported to share the paranormal experiences of others at the Hotel Cecil.

One poster claims to have been in bed at night, when they

suddenly heard the sound of rustling coming from somewhere in the room, as if somebody was going through a bag. The room had already raised this poster's hackles, as it was unusually cold and had a bad atmosphere. They go on to describe experiencing a weight on their chest and a choking sensation that sound very similar to those reported by Patrick Johnston — some forty-six years before.

A second poster reports that their aunt experienced something similar, although this time, while the strange rustling sound and feeling of something heavy on their chest were the same, there is no mention of a feeling of strangulation. Whatever was troubling her aunt stopped when she cried out for help.

It's possible that there are more accounts out there of a similar nature, but let's examine the three that we have.

Three people visit the same hotel, which has hundreds of rooms, and all report a sensation of something pressing heavily down on their chest while they are lying in bed, in some degree of sleep. Two of them hear the sound of something rustling in their room, while one doesn't. Two of them feel as if they are being strangled, while again, one doesn't.

Explanation A: the hotel is haunted, and an intelligent

entity of some sort is seeking out guests to choke while they sleep...alternatively, the residual after-echo of a murder is still being picked up by visitors decades after it happened.

Explanation B: a not uncommon medical condition known as sleep paralysis explains everything, including the rustling in the room (auditory hallucinations), the paralysis, and the choking sensation.

Ockham's Razor clearly steers us toward explanation B, the simplest of the two. Without further evidence, it's the one I'm inclined to go with. And yet, one thing still nags at me. Assuming that the desk clerk's story about a murder having taken place in Patrick Johnston's room was correct, and the clerk wasn't simply playing games with Patrick for his own amusement, then we truly must have one hell of a coincidence. The sort of coincidence which, for me at least, makes the paranormal explanation the simpler one. After all, there were almost seven hundred rooms at the Cecil. The chances of being given Pigeon Goldie's room instead of all the others are poor — very poor.

But not impossible.

So, what does Patrick's daughter think?

"My father *did* experience nightmares," she recalls. "He was prone to them as a child. They could be very vivid and frightening. He would yell, moan and groan in his sleep. My mom would have to go shake him awake."

Her father suffered one recurring nightmare, in which a shadowy figure in dark clothes was chasing him, implying that some kind of harm would befall him if he was ever caught. Crucially, those nightmares never involved a sensation of anything pushing down on his chest, smothering him, or choking him. Those particular feelings were unique to his experience at the Hotel Cecil.

"The other thing that stands out to me is his retelling of the story," Joy goes on. "Even decades later, when he told that story, he became very animated and broke out into a sweat as he relived it. You could clearly see that he was experiencing that fear all over again, thirty-plus years later."

Joy raises a good point. During the process of reliving a past trauma, the human body often reacts as if it is physically undergoing those events all over again. The heart rate and blood pressure go up. Adrenaline floods the body. The mouth goes dry. Sweat begins to form. That doesn't happen to somebody telling a tall story, because practically nobody is that good an actor.

Patrick had that physiologic response every time he told the story, a period which spanned decades, right up until the time he developed dementia. He became so worked up that Joy's mother dreaded the retelling, knowing that she would have her work cut out for her trying to calm her husband down again. Yet he felt compelled to tell it, no matter how painful an experience it was for him to relive, as though trying to make sense of something inexplicable that had haunted him for more than half of his life.

"My dad was not really an emotional man, so for him to have that excess of emotion was really unique for him." To put it into some kind of perspective, Joy relates that as a boy, her father survived the Luftwaffe blitzing the city of Belfast, where he grew up, and had to run to the air raid shelter in order to escape the German bombs. Even when he retold *that* story, he didn't get agitated. In Patrick Johnston's mind, whatever it was that happened to him in that hotel room was more terrifying than being attacked with incendiaries dropped by bombers.

In light of that, it's hard to believe he was making it up, or exaggerating for effect. Could this have simply been a one-off, extremely vivid dream? Sure it could. But how great a coincidence would it be to have such a dream in one of the only rooms out of 700 in which a murder by choking had taken place?

"Perhaps the desk clerk was making fun of my dad," Joy speculates. That's possible, certainly. But you're not going to keep your hotel job for long if you play bad taste pranks on the guests like that, especially when they're deeply upset and agitated, as Patrick Johnston was in the immediate aftermath of his disturbing experience.

The fact of the matter is, as with so many things concerning the Cecil, we will never know for certain what the truth really is.

"To my father, this was absolutely one hundred percent real," Joy concludes. "He never described it as a ghost, or an evil spirit, but he also didn't say it was probably just a nightmare. He was not one to tell tall tales or anything like that.

Speaking for myself, I find Patrick Johnston to be a very credible witness, one with no reason to lie or exaggerate. There was simply nothing in it for him. For the rest of his life, although his nightmares continued, he did not experience sleep paralysis, or anything remotely like what happened to him at the Hotel Cecil that night.

Joy tells me that when it was released, he found Stanley Kubrick's film adaption of Stephen King's *The Shining* to be particularly fascinating. When it comes to his stay at the

Cecil, however, it seems that truth really was stranger than fiction.

I encourage you to seek out Joy's book, *The Reluctant Caregiver,* and visit her online at www.thememoriesproject.com, where you can read her account of her father's chilling experience at the Cecil for yourself.

[https://memoriesproject.com/2012/02/23/dads-stay-at-the-haunted-hotel/]

[https://memoriesproject.com/2021/02/10/my-fathers-cecil-hotel-experience-haunted-him-for-life/]

CHAPTER TEN
The Investigator

Rob Hernandez has spent the better part of the last thirty-six years involved with the paranormal in some way, shape, or form. As a boy, he believes that he came face to face with an apparition one night while going to bed. The experience caused young Rob a great deal of anxiety, and it wasn't the first time he'd seen something he couldn't explain. Just four years old, he saw the figure of a man wearing a coat with long tails. He says that he instinctively knew that this wasn't a flesh and blood human being. Ever since those boyhood encounters, he has been on a personal journey to uncover the truth about the paranormal.

As he grew to adulthood, that passion for all things ghostly only intensified. Rob spends his time investigating claims of hauntings, and he takes great satisfaction in helping people come to terms with the strange things that are going on in their homes. He is particularly fascinated with spirit boxes, the radio frequency sweeping devices that some believe are capable of communicating with the other side, and he custom builds them to order.

Rob is also one of those paranormal investigators who had

the opportunity to visit the Cecil when it was still open to the public and experience the place for himself.

"Ever since *Ghost Adventures* showed up there, the Cecil has become a hot topic, and now nobody can get in," Rob says, "but back in the day, when I first investigated there, you could just walk in off the street, get a room, and do your own research."

He's right. At the time of writing, the hotel is closed and locked up. Things started to change after the death of Elisa Lam made news headlines around the world. Perhaps unwilling to court more negative press, or maybe in a sincere effort to clean up the hotel's reputation, management stopped allowing hotel guests to take visitors up to their room.

Rob's first stay at the Cecil took place in 2011. A small group of his friends wanted to stay there because they were intrigued by Cecil's dark history. For his part, Rob had always wanted to investigate there, and said that he'd like to tag along. He agreed to keep his paranormal investigation low-key, to avoid spooking any of the other guests or residents.

After checking in, they decided to wander around the hotel, just checking things out and generally getting a feel for the place. The trip was a relatively uneventful one, although Rob did hear what could have been disembodied voices. He is quick to point out, however, that it could also have been ambient sounds, rather than paranormal in nature.

When he returned for another visit, it was after the death of Elisa Lam. The atmosphere at the Cecil seemed to have changed a little. For one thing, music was being piped into the corridors and hallways. Rob asked a member of the hotel staff about the reasons behind it, and he was told that the hotel did not want people coming around trying to pick up EVPs. In other words, it was an attempt to deter para-tourists and ghost hunters. I can't help but wonder whether it might also have been designed to try and muffle the sound of sirens, screaming, banging, and other worrisome noises that had been the background soundtrack at the Cecil for many years.

Rob was told that visitors — often people who were not actually staying at the hotel — had started to come upstairs, conduct EVP sessions in the corridors, and bug the paying guests. It seemed to have been decided that enough was enough.

Later that night, Rob and his companions went to the top floor and tried the door which led out onto the roof. A warning sign said that the door was alarmed. It was a commonly held belief that the alarm wasn't actually hooked up to anything. Rob tried the door.

The alarm went off.

The door wasn't locked. It swung open. They could see the rooftop beyond it, and the cloudy Los Angeles night sky. There was some quick discussion about actually going out onto the roof, but with the alarm sounding and somebody from the hotel staff presumably on the way up to check it out, they decided that discretion was the better part of valor, and so retreated to a safe (and presumably deniable) distance.

It took half an hour for anybody to come and investigate. When they did, the staff member simply pulled the door shut. They didn't seem overly bothered about who had opened it up, or why.

When the time had come to book the rooms, Rob had made a big mistake. Calling the hotel, he inadvertently mentioned his interest in the paranormal. He was just trying to make conversation. The employee at the other end of the line promptly hung up on him.

Lesson learned. The next time he called to make a booking, he made no mention of ghosts. It seemed like the safest thing to do.

For Rob, the most awe-inspiring part of the hotel was its lobby. Many visitors have observed that stepping through the Cecil's front doors is like walking back into a bygone age. A pinstripe suit-wearing gangster would not look out of place in there, with a cigarette holder in hand and a flapper girl on his arm. The intricate painted glass ceiling above, the gleaming tile floor below, and the intricate decor all around seem more suited to the 1930s than the 21st century.

"I had made a conscious effort to clear my mind before I went in," he explains. "That's what I do at any supposedly haunted location. I don't read up on the history. I don't do too much background research, because I don't want to bias myself. I just said to myself, *Rob, this is just an old hotel. Let's walk on inside and see what we see.*"

The grandeur of the lobby took him by surprise, particularly considering the squalor which he had passed through in order to reach the hotel.

"On the outside, it looks like hell, but when you walk inside and see that art deco, it's like, *oh my God...*"

Rob and one of his friends were staying in Room 1419 that night, which was said to have been the room from which Richard Ramirez blasted out his music at a constant, near-deafening volume. The other two members of their group stayed in Pigeon Goldie Osgood's former room. One would be tempted to think that if any rooms at the Cecil were paranormally active, then these would be the two.

That wasn't necessarily the case.

So, what did the Night Stalker's room feel like? Was the atmosphere heavy and oppressive? Was there a lingering sense of darkness, the stain left behind by a truly twisted and evil man, one who was now dead — perhaps a dark and foreboding air of menace?

No.

"It just felt like any other hotel room," Rob muses matter-of-factly. "I didn't feel anything else."

That's a breath of fresh air. One would expect Rob to have been prejudiced about sleeping in a room with such a negative association. To be frank, as I interview him, I'm expecting to hear a string of the usual cliches. To instead be told that Richard Ramirez's room was, at best, unremarkable, is refreshing, to say the least.

Except perhaps not a literal breath of fresh air. "The room smelled *terrible*," Rob chuckles. "Old, musty, and dirty. The room was clean, at least, but if you sat on the bed, you ran the danger of getting bedbugs. We were warned about that, in fact." Warned by a friend, not by the hotel staff, Rob and his companion pulled all of the bedding off the mattress, dumped it onto the floor and laid out sleeping bags on the bed; although he came through unscathed, she was bitten by bedbugs on both of her arms and legs. They put their sleeping bags in a trash bag after they checked out.

After running the faucets for a minute or two, he learned that even the Cecil's water had a unique, sulfurous odor to it. Nobody felt comfortable showering in the stuff, let alone drinking it. This was true even before the body of Elisa Lam contaminated the water supply, and it was consistent on all of Rob's visits.

With two of the hotel's more notorious rooms at their disposal, Rob's group elected to try a couple of ghost box sessions. These are essentially radio frequency hopping devices which scan quickly from one frequency to the next, emitting short bursts of static and occasionally, snippets of voices. Some paranormal enthusiasts claim that the dead can use this method to communicate with the living; skeptics, on the other hand, counter with the argument that all that the listener hears is random sound bites from commercial radio stations, and audio pareidolia — the phenomenon by which our brain attempts to make sense out of jumbled sound, and essentially tricks us into perceiving meaning where there is actually none.

In this case, nothing meaningful came through during any of the ghost box sessions. The EVP sessions bore slightly more fruit, but again, Rob freely admits that the voices they recorded could have been noise contamination from guests in neighboring rooms, or from the neighborhood outside. Seasoned investigators obey the rule: *If in doubt, throw it out,* when it pertains to potential evidence of the paranormal. In other words, if there's reasonable doubt about the nature of any given finding, you have to dismiss it out of hand. It's simply the prudent and ethical thing to do.

In both rooms, there was little in the way of quiet to be had. The sound of neighbors drifted through the walls, which seemed to be paper thin. There were also bursts of raucous noise from further down the hallway. Any audio recordings made in such an uncontrolled environment must be deemed dubious from the very beginning.

In terms of gathering evidence, the Hotel Cecil investigation was a complete wash. Nor did any of the group have any personal experiences of a strange nature; nobody was touched, experienced cold spots or drafts, or underwent any physical symptoms on any of Rob's investigations.

Rob made attempts to speak with the staff in order to ask them about their own experiences, but found them to be, in his own words, "very standoffish." Whenever he's conducting a paranormal investigation in a hotel, Rob makes a point of trying to connect with a janitor or cleaner to gather a little history about their workplace. During his stays at the Cecil, he didn't even *see* any of the hotel staff, with the sole exception of the desk clerk who checked him in, and the person who responded to the tripped alarm on the rooftop door.

Encountering a male member of staff in the lobby, Rob approached him and tried to spark up a conversation. The man immediately grew defensive as Rob started asking questions, clamming up and refusing to talk about happenings at the hotel. Even the bartender wasn't inclined to talk. To an extent, that's understandable. The Cecil didn't have the greatest reputation at that point, and it would be in the hotel's best interests for its staff to not answer any questions about its darker side. After all, what good could come of it?

I ask Rob whether he's aware of any credible evidence that the Cecil is haunted — or at least, as haunted as some people have claimed.

"I don't think that there is," he responds without hesitation. He adds that in his view, far too many people are willing to accept at face value the idea that a hotel with a background as grim as the Cecil's simply *must* be haunted. In fact, not just haunted, but practically *infested* with negative entities.

He and I agree that the hotel almost certainly has its ghosts, but by the same token, it is nowhere near the portal to Hell that it has often been made out to be in various media portrayals.

"Is there dark energy there? Maybe. But I think a lot of this comes down to the environment around the hotel: Skid Row. I think that all of the drug use, the prostitution, the mental illness that takes place out there is tied to what happens at the Cecil. That visitors to the hotel are picking up on it."

It's an interesting theory. "So, let me ask you this," I counter. "Let's say that hypothetically, this same hotel was located in, say, New York City. A totally different neighborhood. Would strange things still be reported there?"

What I'm really asking, of course, is whether he thinks that the Cecil's cursed and haunted reputation is a product of its own history, or of its location on Skid Row.

"It's absolutely the location. Even the surrounding buildings have that same weird energy. I've been into some of the other buildings in that neighborhood, and the energy feels exactly the same — it's not just the Cecil."

I can't help thinking of The Last Bookstore, not far from the hotel. It's the place where Elisa Lam stopped off to buy books when she was staying at the Cecil. The store also has a reputation for being haunted. Coincidence, or a product of the same energy that Rob thinks is affecting the Cecil and the local area?

Rob's keen to differentiate between the concepts of *energy* and *haunting*. They aren't necessarily the same thing, he says, although the two things are often interconnected.

"Do you believe that any of the suicides which took place there could have been influenced by this weird energy?" I ask.

"Absolutely. Have you ever walked into a location and suddenly gotten very emotional, for no apparent reason?"

I nod. That has happened to me rarely, but I've seen it happen to others quite often, especially at locations associated with a lot of tragedy.

"I think in those cases, you're picking up on somebody else's emotions," Rob continues. "Some people can be pushed over the edge by that. Especially if they're susceptible."

It's certainly food for thought. I'm not necessarily convinced that those poor folks who took their own lives at the Cecil were pushed into doing so by some sort of unseen energy...but I'm not willing to rule it out either.

Thinking ahead, it's reasonable to assume that if Rob is correct about strange energies tainting the neighborhood, then things aren't likely to change when the Cecil re-opens in its newest incarnation, which is supposed to happen later in 2021. Changing the interior, the fixtures, the fittings, even the plumbing and wiring, isn't going to change the location. It will be worth keeping an eye on the building at 640 S. Main, if for no other reason than to see what the next generation of residents and guests report experiencing.

"It's one big psychic scar," Rob concludes. "You could demolish the entire building, and it wouldn't make a difference. You're still going to have that energy there, and it isn't going away."

Considering the sheer volume of negative events that have taken place in and around the Hotel Cecil for the past few decades, I would consider it truly remarkable if strange things *weren't* taking place there. As I said at the very beginning: almost all hotels have their ghosts. Why should the Cecil be any different?

At the same time, I find it likely that the connection with Richard Ramirez has been vastly overplayed. Some claim that he performed occult rituals on the roof. If that's true — and I'm not certain whether it is or it isn't — then it's possible that some kind of negative energy or entity was conjured up, as Zak Bagans hypothesized. Ramirez did have a deep and abiding interest in Devil worship, believing that Satan watched over him and acted as his protector.

On the other hand, it would be imprudent of us to simply take that assumption at face value. Ramirez, by all accounts, spent a lot of time in his room, stoned, listening to loud music. We have no actual proof that he spent time dabbling in occult practices at the Cecil, let alone carry out rituals on the roof; what we do have is conjecture and hearsay.

As the final chapter of this book closes out, it is worth noting that a new chapter is about to begin for the Hotel Cecil. Once its doors open again, the hotel will have gotten a facelift. Its interior will gleam anew, fresh paint, new fixtures and fittings. Perhaps some semblance of the glory days will come back, when tourists and residents with money to spend come back, and along with them will come an influx of positive energy.

Yet the hotel's bones will remain the same. At its heart, no matter what name it goes by, the building at 640 South Main will always be the Hotel Cecil.

Can a leopard really change its spots...?

Only time will tell.

Acknowledgments

Firstly, to you, the reader: Thank you for spending your hard-earned money and valuable time in order to read this book. It is my sincere hope that you have enjoyed it, and I would ask you to please consider rating the book on Amazon's website. In the current writing market, books tend to live and die by their reviews and ratings, particularly on Amazon. Your help would therefore be greatly appreciated.

The author would like to extend his sincerest thanks to the following people, without whom this book would not have been possible.

Kari K. Miller, the mother-in-law I never met, and Laura, for allowing me to share her story.

Rob Hernandez and Joy Johnston , for graciously sharing their experiences and opinions with me.

My supporters:
- MJ Dickson
- Kirsten Honey

- Ellen MacNeil
- Linda Corbet
- Chris Sutton
- Shannon Byers
- Andrew Arthurton
- Linda Dix
- Patrizia Charping
- Brian Corey
- Cindy Fritz
- Mo Keohan
- Angela Tofflemire
- Judy Regini
- Ashley Wiseman
- Rachel Vore Engle
- Michael Sebille
- Kayte Robbins
- Jim Sturgill
- Luke Summey

I truly appreciate your support – thank you!

Much love,
Richard

Printed in Great Britain
by Amazon